PASTOR to PASTOR

PASTOR to PASTOR

TACKLING PROBLEMS OF THE PULPIT

by

ERWIN W. LUTZER

MOODY PRESS

CHICAGO

To those who share the responsibilities
of pastoral ministry with me at Moody Church:

Grant Anderson
David Craig
Paul Craig
Richard Duncan
Gerald Edmonds
Matthew Heard
Bruce Jones

© 1987 by
THE MOODY BIBLE INSTITUTE
OF CHICAGO

All Scripture quotations, unless noted otherwise, are from the *New American
Standard Bible,* © 1960, 1962, 1963, 1968, 1971, 1972, 1973, 1975, and 1977 by
The Lockman Foundation, and are used by permission.

Illustrations by Joe DeVelasco

Library of Congress Cataloging in Publication Data

Lutzer, Erwin W.
    Pastor to pastor.

    1. Clergy—Office.   2. Pastoral theology.   I. Title.
BV660.2.L87   1987   253   87-7854
ISBN 0-8024-6326-6

1 2 3 4 5 Printing/DP/Year 91 90 89 88 87

Printed in the United States of America

Contents

Foreword

Numerous books are available to guide us as we face and solve personal and church problems. I have read many of those books and have found them helpful in one way or another.

Then, why another one?

Because this one aims for a much higher goal than simply the answering of questions or the solving of problems.

Personal spiritual growth: that is Erwin Lutzer's great concern as he shares these insights with you. The goal is not just the solving of church problems, as important as that is, but the spiritual development of both minister and congregation. After all, each problem we encounter is an opportunity for both pastor and people to face the situation honestly, seek God's wisdom diligently, and obey His will trustingly. The result? Spiritual growth all around!

Something else makes these chapters unique: they come from the heart and mind of a man who is a pastor, theologian, teacher, and philosopher, a man who has a heart for revival and renewal in the church. Erwin Lutzer draws from a wealth of learning that has been filtered through the grid of personal experience. No ivory tower ideas here—and no pious evasions!

Don't speed-read this book. Pause, ponder, pray—and grow!

WARREN W. WIERSBE
General Director
Back to the Bible
Lincoln, Nebraska

He only needs twelve!

1

The Call to the Ministry:
Do We Need One?

Suppose Charles Spurgeon and Billy Graham had chosen careers other than preaching. Would it have been all the same to God?

I don't think so. Though the idea is not popular today, I believe God still calls individuals to specific ministries, particularly preaching and teaching His Word.

During the past twenty years, missionaries have been telling us that there is no need for a specific call. Christ commanded us to preach the gospel; so, if we qualify, we should go. Don't waste time waiting for a signal from heaven.

In *Decision Making and the Will of God* (Multnomah, 1981), Garry Friesen teaches that God has a sovereign will (His overall plan) and a moral will (His guidelines for life and belief) but no individual plan for every believer.

He asks us to remember how difficult it was to "find the will of God" when we had to make a particular decision and explains why that happened: we were looking for something that did not exist.

Friesen exhorts us to make decisions on the basis of wisdom. Gather all the information you can, weigh the pros and cons, and make your own decision in faith.

What about all the men called by God in the Scriptures? he asks. Because God spoke audibly, they had no doubt as to His will for them. But He doesn't do that today, so those examples don't apply. We're expected to be obedient to God's moral will, but after that the decisions are ours. Any one of a number of choices would be fine with God.

There's some truth in that. Many of us grew up thinking we had to pry into the secret counsels of God whenever we had a decision to make. We tried to read His diary, but the print seemed blurred. His will was a mystery wrapped in an enigma. Doubtless we should have just gone ahead and made a reasonable decision.

We also believed that a Damascus-road experience was needed to be called to the ministry. Short of that, we felt obligated to choose a "secular" vocation.

Furthermore, emphasizing a call to the ministry tends to exaggerate the distinction between clergy and laity. Every believer is a minister of God. To say that some Christians are called to specific ministries while others aren't seems contrary to the biblical teaching that each member of the Body of Christ is important.

Friesen's position would also explain why some have felt called to ministries for which they were ill-suited. Put simply, they were mistaken. What they thought was the Holy Spirit's leading was nothing but a personal hunch. You may have heard about the man who was called to preach; unfortunately, no one was called to listen.

The guidance of the Spirit. What about the personal ministry of the Holy Spirit in a believer's life? Spurgeon and Graham, along with hundreds of other preachers, have said that they chose the ministry only because God chose them for it.

Apparently Timothy didn't have an audible call. Yet I can't imagine Paul's telling him that he could leave the ministry if he wished without leaving the will of God. On the contrary, Paul urged him to fulfill his ministry.

I don't see how anyone could survive in the ministry if he felt it was just his own choice. Some ministers scarcely have two good days back to back. They are sustained by the knowledge that God has placed them where they are. Ministers without such a conviction often lack courage and carry their resignation letter in their coat pocket. At the slightest hint of difficulty, they're gone.

I'm disturbed by those who preach and teach without a sense of calling. Those who consider the ministry to be one choice among many tend to have horizontal vision. They lack the urgency of Paul, who said, "Necessity is laid upon me."

John Jowett says, "If we lose the sense of wonder of our commission, we shall become like common traders in a common market, babbling about common wares" (*The Preacher, His Life and Work* [Grand Rapids: Baker, 1968], p. 21).

Since God called numerous individuals to specific ministries in Bible times, it is only logical that He would do so today. Though He doesn't call audibly anymore, now that the New Testament is complete we have an adequate basis to test the inner guidance of the Spirit.

What a call means. Let me risk my own definition of a call: God's call is an inner conviction given by the Holy Spirit and confirmed by the Word of God and the Body of Christ.

Notice the three parts to the definition. First, it is an inner conviction. Feelings and hunches come and go. They may be based on impressions we had as children when we romanticized the idea of becoming a missionary. Or maybe we idolized the role of a pastor.

But God-given compulsion is not deterred by obstacles. It gives the single-mindedness needed for effective ministry.

Of course, we don't all have to be called the same way. Circumstances and temperaments vary. For some, the conviction may be sudden; for others, gradual. A person may sense no call at all until encouraged by discerning members of the Body of Christ. Yet despite those differences, there is a sense of purpose. Woe is me if I preach not the gospel!

Second, the Word of God must confirm it. We have to ask whether a person has the qualifications listed in 1 Timothy 3. Is he mature? Does he have the gifts needed? Has he labored in the

Word of God in doctrine? Or might he have disqualified himself through moral or doctrinal compromise?

No doubt mistakes have been made when the scriptural qualifications have been overlooked in deference to a call. If a man says he's called, that has seemed to be reason enough to thrust him into ministry. But the Word of God should be used to confirm his inner compulsion.

If the man fails the test of the Scriptures, he must be excluded from ministry. Perhaps at a later time his call can be realized.

Third, the Body of Christ helps us understand where we fit within the local church framework. The Body enables its members to find their spiritual gifts and is a testing ground for further ministry. Those who are faithful in the least may later be entrusted with greater responsibility.

My own ministry was confirmed when my pastor asked me to preach occasionally when I was in Bible school. The affirmation I received confirmed what I believed to be the leading of the Spirit within my heart and mind.

Often a person senses a call to the ministry but has no leading to a particular organization or church. God often uses the Body of Christ or, in the case of a missionary, a mission board to clarify the next step.

Though the details are different in each case, the end result must be the same: a sense of the divine initiative, a commission that leaves a man or woman with a settled assurance that he or she is doing what God desires.

Jowett perhaps overstated it only slightly when he wrote, "The call of the Eternal must ring through the rooms of his soul as clearly as the sound of the morning-bell rings through the valleys of Switzerland, calling the peasants to early prayer and praise"(*The Preacher, His life and Work,* p. 12).

Spurgeon discouraged men from entering the ministry. He told them plainly that if they could take another vocation they should. He wanted only those who felt strongly that they had no other alternative. They were called of God.

How do I explain those who have dropped out of the ministry? Should they feel as if they have failed in their calling? Of course, it's possible that some have. That doesn't mean God can't use them in other vocations, for He is always working in spite of our failures.

But there may be other explanations. Perhaps they were called, but the Body of Christ failed them. Young men have been ruined by critical congregations.

Others may not have failed at all, but worldly standards of success would interpret their ministry that way. We would have considered Isaiah's ministry a failure.

Then again, some may be like John Mark; discouraged, they give up at first, but they may become effective in a later ministry.

We do not know all of the contingencies, but let us not allow those difficulties to rid us of a divine sense of calling that gives us our courage and authority.

your Dad's a minister?
what does he do the
rest of the time?

2
A Congregation's Expectations:
Can We Adjust?

"**I**f you have the reputation of being an early riser, you can sleep till noon."

I don't remember where I read this bit of insight, but it reminded me that a congregation's perception of its pastor influences for good or for ill the effectiveness of his ministry. If he's perceived as dishonest or inept or as one who cannot keep a confidence, his words and actions will be interpreted through a negative grid; if he's thought of as godly and competent, he will be given the benefit of the doubt even when he fails.

Often, this situation puts him at a disadvantage. If he should lose the congregation's goodwill, his ministry might soon be over. But if he consciously attempts to establish and maintain a correct impression, he courts spiritual disaster.

Pressures of public ministry. Pastors are constantly open to public evaluation. Preach nine good messages and one blooper, and some will remember only the one that bombed. Walk past a deacon without acknowledging him, and you might rankle his feelings. And if a disgruntled church member begins some gossip, a little leaven could leaven the whole lump.

We're also under pressure because few members of the congregation know the demands of our schedules.

One pastor asked his deacons to outline how they thought he spent his time. They had difficulty coming up with a forty-hour week, though he was working seventy.

We've all laughed at the child who says to the pastor's kid, "My dad isn't like yours—he works for a living." But it hurts just the same.

Once you've gained a reputation, you're more or less stuck with it. I read about a pastor who was at a baseball game when a church member needed him. The irate parishioner spread the story that the pastor spent all his time at the ballpark. The pastor nearly ruined his health and family working overtime to correct the false impression. Even so, it lingered.

Such perceptions, whether true or false, can wield awesome authority over us. If we are self-conscious, always wondering how well we are liked, we'll soon be a slave to the pulse of our popularity. Everything will be done with an eye on our ratings.

At that point, we'll lose our authority to minister. "The fear of man brings a snare" (Proverbs 29:25). We'll desire to remain neutral in disputes, trying earnestly to agree with everyone. Church discipline will not be administered for fear of criticism. We'll back away from any unpopular stand, even when it's right.

I'm not saying we should be insensitive. We've all met the pastor who takes pride in "not caring what anyone thinks," callously disregarding the feelings of others. I'm talking about a lack of boldness even in matters that are scripturally clear.

We'll also find it difficult to rejoice in the success of other pastors. Television has brought the super church to our parishioners' living rooms. Comparison is inevitable.

We may even take secret delight in another's failure. One assistant pastor, who was an apparent threat to the senior pastor, told me, "Nothing would delight him more than if I were to blow it."

When we're overly sensitive to what others think, we'll also live with guilt—the nagging feeling that we could be doing more. Since by definition our work is never finished, we then carry it home with us. My wife would tell you that sometimes I'm not at home even when I'm physically present. I'm preoccupied with the pressures of the day and the ones I'll face tomorrow.

In the process, our faith is eroded. Christ directed this question to the Pharisees: "How can you believe, when you receive glory from one another, and you do not seek the glory that is from the one and only God?" (John 5:44). The desire for human praise and the faith to minister cancel each other—seek the one and the other eludes you.

When in conflict with the Pharisees who were somewhat less than enthusiastic about His ministry, Jesus said, "And He who sent Me is with Me; He has not left Me alone, for I always do the things that are pleasing to Him" (John 8:29).

Freedom to serve. Our Lord was free from men's opinions about Him. Though He cared what they thought, because He had the words of eternal life, His actions were never calculated to gain their praise. The will of the Father was all that mattered. And if the Father was pleased, the Son was pleased.

I've known pastors like that—surrendered, secure, and free from actions motivated by a desire for human praise. No need to prove themselves or be in the limelight. No grudging admissions about other people's successes—just freedom and joy in the work of the Lord.

What characteristics could we expect if we were brought to such a place of surrender?

First, we would not let people push us into their mold. We all live with the tension between what we are versus what others want us to be. We'd like to fulfill the exalted expectations that many people may have for us, but we can't. If we know ourselves realistically, both our strengths and weaknesses, we'll not think that we are God's gift to every human need.

Christ faced this tension, too. After He fed the multitude, the crowd sought to crown Him king. But He went off by Himself, refusing to consider the offer even though He knew that He was a disappointment to His followers. His miracles generated expectations He simply could not fulfill at the time.

Yet before His death He could say He had finished the Father's work, though hundreds of people were still sick and thousands more had not believed on Him. But the pressure of those needs did not blur His vision to please the Father only.

The more blessed people are by our ministry, the greater their expectations of us will be. If we let them, they will lead us to believe that we're the only ones who can lead people to Christ, counsel the emotionally troubled, or visit in the hospital.

And if we believe that we are God's answer to every need, we'll also accept every invitation for lunch, attend all committee meetings, and take outside speaking engagements when asked —all at the expense of our families, our health, and, most of all, our relationship with God.

Let's not let our successes propel us into a role that is beyond our strengths and abilities. Our self-image must always be adjusted to fit reality. Saying no graciously is an essential characteristic of a man who has submitted his will to God.

Second, we would profit from criticism. No one likes criticism, particularly when it's unfair. Furthermore, we usually don't get a chance to give our side of the story without risking additional misunderstanding.

Yet sometimes, even when the criticism is valid, our pride prevents us from learning during the experience. When we think of ourselves more highly than we ought to think, we may believe we are beyond rebuke.

Paul also received criticism. He was under fire for going to the Gentiles and was imprisoned because he refused to compromise the inclusive claim of the gospel.

Sometimes the condemnation was personal and vindictive: "His letters are weighty and strong, but his personal presence is unimpressive, and his speech contemptible" (2 Corinthians 10:10). But he was undeterred. He knew that God would vindicate him.

Every leader has his critics. If we are especially sensitive, if we cannot tolerate differences of opinion and refuse to learn from criticism, we're still clinging to our reputations.

Many lies were published about revivalist George Whitefield to discourage the crowds from hearing him, but he responded by saying that he could wait until God rendered the final judgment. Such a man of faith cannot be destroyed.

Third, we would not be afraid to let our humanity show. Our congregations believe that we are different—free from the emotional and spiritual struggles of others. After all, if we are not walking in uninterrupted victory, who is there left to lean on? Heroes are in short supply, and a pastor who has been a blessing to his flock is a good candidate to fulfill the role.

If we refuse to talk about our failures and share only our victories, we'll reinforce that distorted perception. Eventually, it will give way to myth.

One pastor confessed in exhaustion, "My congregation expects me to be perfect."

Our lack of authenticity creates a burden that is too heavy to bear. Struggling under its weight, we'll assume we have indeed arrived spiritually and hence be blind to our shortcomings or kill ourselves trying to live up to others' expectations. We'll also tend to withdraw, fearful that people will get to know what we're really like.

Yet, what pastor hasn't done some things he's ashamed of? If our congregations could open our minds for inspection, we'd all resign in shame and disgrace.

We can help our people better when we let them know that we stand with them in the quest for righteousness, neither above nor off to the side where the arrows of Satan and the passions of the flesh can't touch us. Honesty communicates much better than a false sense of perfection.

A letter written to a pastor by a member of his congregation said in part, "Are you as human as we are? Have you struggled with some of the same problems we face during the week? Is there discord in your home? Heartache? Anguish? Won't you share that with us, too, as you share your doctrine, your theology, your exposition?"

Finally, we would not see the success of another as a threat to our own ministry.

When the Holy Spirit came upon the seventy elders during the ministry of Moses, two men continued to prophesy. Joshua, jealous for Moses' reputation, suggested that Moses restrain them.

But Moses replied, "Are you jealous for my sake? Would that all the Lord's people were prophets, that the Lord would put His Spirit upon them!" (Numbers 11:29).

Here was a man who could rejoice in the success of others. He did not want to keep his gift to himself, nor did he have to defend his call to the ministry.

Many pastors struggle over the success of another, especially if that individual is on the same staff. The fact that God sometimes uses those who are less gifted, or even less authentic than we would like, brings the sin of envy to the surface.

But the person who has died to himself will bow humbly, resisting the temptation to be envious simply because God is generous.

In the parable of the workers in the vineyard, the landowner said to those who had worked longer hours and grumbled about equal pay, "Is it not lawful for me to do what I wish with what is my own? Or is your eye envious because I am generous?" (Matthew 20:15).

It's God's prerogative to bless some people more than He should. Apart from such grace we'd all be lost.

Friends of John the Baptist were concerned because some of his disciples were leaving to follow Christ.

John responded, "A man can receive nothing, unless it has been given him from heaven" (John 3:27). If we believed those words, we'd be free from all comparisons, competition, and self-consciousness in the ministry. We'd serve with a glad heart, accepting our role.

Later, John added, "He must increase, but I must decrease" (John 3:30).

Even if our ministry should be diminished, we can accept it more easily if Christ is honored through submission to His will.

Since it is God-given, we can take no credit for it nor can we insist that it continue.

If we have become men-pleasers, let's repent. Such an attitude is an affront to God. Subtly, we are preaching ourselves, not Christ.

If you have the reputation of being an early riser, you can sleep till noon. But God knows when you get out of bed, and His perception is the one that really counts.

3

Surviving a Skirmish:
How Should We Relate to the Board?

Perhaps the most sensitive pressure point in a church organization is the relationship between the pastor and the church board. The details differ, but the story is the same: the pastor wants to take the church one direction, the board another.

The pastor believes he receives his orders from God so the board had better follow him. But the board is unconvinced and digs in its heels, settling down for a long power struggle.

Division can come over anything from the building program to the order of the morning worship service. Pastors and boards have parted company over whether wine should be served for Communion, divorced people should teach in Sunday school, or the carpet should be blue or red.

The issue is often irrelevant. It's who wins that counts. What's at stake is power, and the question of who's in charge must be settled. Eventually it will be, but often at the expense of a split.

As pastors, we sometimes bring division on ourselves. For some, submitting to the board is a sign of weakness, a denial of a God-given mandate. Some of us think that to be called of God is a guarantee that we know God's will for our congregations. Furthermore, we may think that God blesses only those pastors who stand up for their views regardless of the cost.

The more dictatorial the pastor, the more necessary it seems for him to win on every issue. He interprets even minor matters as a referendum on his leadership, so he must get his way every time. And if the board doesn't grant his wish, he'll resort to pressure, bypassing the board to appeal to the congregation or coercing other leaders in the church.

Such a pastor may not realize that what he gains in the power struggle, he loses in credibility and respect.

Peter had a different understanding of the elder's role: "Shepherd the flock of God among you, exercising oversight not under compulsion, but voluntarily, according to the will of God; and not for sordid gain, but with eagerness; nor yet as lording it over those allotted to your charge, but proving to be examples to the flock" (1 Peter 5:2-3).

Christ taught that the primary quality of leadership was servanthood, not a dictatorial spirit. The Gentiles sought superiority and control; believers should seek humility and submission. The only clear instance of one-man rule in the New Testament is that of Diotrephes, who loved to have the preeminence (3 John 9).

I'm not suggesting, however, that the board is always innocent. I've heard many horror stories of church boards that have driven their pastors to unnecessary resignations. But I'd like to suggest some basic principles that can help us in negotiating the inevitable differences that arise.

Everyone on the board (including the pastor) must be subject to the board's consensus. After an exhaustive study of every relevant New Testament passage on the topic, Bruce Stabbert states in his book *The Team Concept:* "In all these passages, there is not one passage which describes a church being governed by one pastor."

Of course, in Baptist polity, deacons usually assume the responsibilities that elders held in the New Testament. The principle of plurality of leadership still applies, regardless of how churches are organized. The pastor, therefore, has no authority to act independently of his board. He cannot override its vote by an appeal to his divine call because all the elders have equal authority. They, too, have a divine call.

Nor should the pastor threaten to resign unless the controversy merits his resignation. More than one board has called a pastor's bluff and forced him to eat his words or follow through with his threat.

But what if the board is obviously wrong? If the matter involves eternal truth, such as important doctrinal or moral issues, the pastor must warn the offending party of the consequences. There are times when a split may be necessary. As the apostle Paul taught, "For there must also be factions among you, in order that those who are approved may have become evident among you" (1 Corinthians 11:19).

But I've seldom heard of a split because of doctrinal or moral error. Usually it's because of the building program, the pastor's leadership style, or floundering church programs.

When difficulties arise, the pastor often feels slighted, unappreciated, and misunderstood. The innate desire we all have to justify ourselves may take over, and the pastor determines that he will not leave until justice is done.

Paul, however, admonishes us not to avenge ourselves, but to let God settle our accounts. Blessed is the pastor-elder who can accept wrong without compromise, but also without retaliation.

However much he may try to convince the board of his viewpoint, the bottom line is that he must submit to its authority unless a clear point of Scripture is at stake. It's better to leave than to stay to prove a point or to get "justice."

The pastor must lead through the board. He must share his vision with those to whom he is accountable. Here is where time and patience bring fruitful dividends—when the board acts as one in making decisions for the benefit of the Body.

But that kind of unity comes only through prayer and hard work. If the previous pastor had a tarnished reputation, it will take time before the board has confidence in the new pastor's integrity. There will be a trial period until mutual confidence is established.

When a decision is made as a body, there is also shared responsibility. Does that mean the pastor shouldn't be a strong leader? Not at all. Most boards expect their pastor to take the initiative, to give the ministry direction. In 1 Timothy 5:17 Paul writes, "Let the elders who rule well be considered worthy of double honor, especially those who work hard at preaching and teaching."

The New Testament allows for strong leadership within the plurality of elders. However, if the pastor dictates to the board, and it is not an integral part of the decision-making process, its members may eventually polarize against him. A board may have diversity of opinion about a proposal, of course. But the pastor and board must be willing to pray and wait until a consensus emerges.

A word of caution: sometimes a board doesn't stand behind its decisions if members voted yes just for the sake of pleasing the pastor or for the sake of unity. The ability to sense whether a board is sold on an idea or just going along for the ride is an art.

The board must keep its members from becoming unruly. This scenario has happened a thousand times: one board member, usually the unofficial "church boss," itches for recognition and control. He begins to oppose the pastor and pretends to speak for others. The other board members are intimidated. *After all,* they reason, *he's been in the church for years, and his wife plays the piano.* So they sit by, hoping the problem will go away. But it only gets worse, and discord spreads.

In one church, an elder ruined the ministry of three pastors by using the same strategy. He would befriend the pastor in the first year and then turn against him in the second. Because of his influence, he'd generate enough opposition to force a showdown. The board was at a loss to deal with the problem, so the members let it go on.

Unfortunately, the board usually believes the pastor is more expendable. Pastors come and go, but the elder stays forever.

The board must have the strength to discipline its own members. If not, church leaders adopt a double standard, and the work of God is hindered.

Paul gives some specific instructions for confronting an elder. An accusation should not be received except on the basis of two or three witnesses, and if an elder continues in sin, he should be rebuked publicly (1 Timothy 5:19-20). The pastor must enlist the cooperation of other board members when calling a fellow elder to accountability.

If Satan can't get a pastor to ruin his own reputation, step two is to create friction between him and the board. Without unity, we can conquer neither the world nor the devil. As Benjamin Franklin said at the signing of the Declaration of Independence, "We must all hang together, or assuredly we shall all hang separately."

Let's redouble our effort to obey Paul's admonition to be "diligent to preserve the unity of the Spirit in the bond of peace" (Ephesians 4:3). Anything less will cause the Body of Christ to work against itself.

If I didn't love you,
I wouldn't even speak
to you!

4

Problem People:
Confrontation or Compromise?

A friend of mine, fresh out of Bible college, became the pastor of a small country church. One day the elders asked him to visit a wealthy member who hadn't been attending regularly but continued to contribute to the church coffers. "We don't think he's even a Christian," they said.

So at their insistence, he visited the old gentleman and asked him point-blank if he was saved. The man became incensed at the pastor's audacity to suggest that he, a self-made man, was not a Christian.

Several weeks later, the church building burned down. The congregation met in a schoolroom to decide what to do. After the decision was made to rebuild, the man whose salvation had been questioned stood up.

"This young man had the nerve to question whether I was a Christian—what do you suggest we do about it?" He sat down with an air of importance, waiting for a response.

Silence.

"I move we terminate him as pastor," the man said.

There was some discussion, but not one of the elders rose to defend their pastor and explain that he had been acting on their request. Later a vote was taken, and the young man was given two weeks to resign.

After the meeting, no one came to speak to him except a school janitor, who heard over the public address system what had happened. The pastor left the building and began walking in blinding rain mile after mile, scarcely aware of where he was going.

That was thirty-five years ago. He never pastored another church.

Techniques of opposition. Most of us haven't had such an experience. But perhaps we've had board members who supported us in meetings but criticized us to others. We've all had to work with people who are negative, critical, and obnoxious. In one church, a man takes notes diligently with the intent of keeping the pastor straight on his theology. After each service he confronts the pastor, explaining how he could improve his preaching.

Recently a pastor told me about a parishioner who opposed his ministry. The critic would approach a member of the congregation and throw him some bait. "You know, I've met people within the congregation who question whether the pastor should . . ." If the person said he strongly supported the pastor, the man would back off. Because he claimed to be speaking for others in the congregation, he faced no personal risk. But if there was some agreement, the critic would sow bitter seeds of discord.

He was a garbage collector. He went from person to person gathering grievances. Eventually he stirred up enough trouble to force the pastor's resignation.

Ironically, sometimes the person who befriends the pastor when he first arrives is the one who later turns against him. The man is attracted to the pastor because he wants to brief him on the way things really are. But if the pastor doesn't agree with him right down the line, he will soon become his adversary. To see the pastor succeed would be his greatest disappointment.

The problem person doesn't see himself as difficult to live with but as a loyal member of the congregation just doing his duty. Many a person like that has sent a pastor to an early grave —either unaware of his destructive influence or sincerely thinking that the pastor deserved to be punished.

What makes it difficult is that most problem people will not face the pastor directly to try to resolve their disagreements. They ignore Christ's teaching about going directly to the person with whom one has a dispute (Matthew 18:15-17). They prefer to give their speech at a public meeting where they can claim to speak for others—and at the same time poison the atmosphere of the whole church. The pastor may find it difficult to defend himself for fear he might be viewed as unspiritual. And even if he does have a legitimate defense, the damage has been done.

Handling dragons. How shall we cope with difficult people in our congregations? First, we must listen carefully to what they are saying—they just may be right. Some pastors are so sensitive to criticism that they tend to reject all negative comments. But even if we think the person has been unfair, there may be some truth to what he has said.

Many a potential problem has been diffused by simply giving our friend an honest hearing. In fact, he may be doing you a favor. "Reprove a wise man, and he will love you" (Proverbs 9:8). Others in the congregation may have the same criticisms, but haven't felt free to tell you. In *Well-Intentioned Dragons* (Carol Stream, Ill.: Christianity Today, 1985), Marshall Shelley writes, "Solitary shots should be ignored, but when they come from several directions, it's time to pay attention. As someone once said, 'If one calls you a donkey, ignore him. If two call you a donkey, check for hoof prints. If three call you a donkey, get a saddle'" (p. 110).

After you've heard him out, you must see the problem in perspective. You can receive a hundred compliments, but it's that one criticism that sticks in your mind. Many a pastor has spent a sleepless night because of a single negative remark.

But now is the time for sober analysis. Is the criticism at least partially correct? Is it because of a difference over style or leadership philosophy, or might it be a personality conflict? If you've hurt someone's feelings, even unintentionally, humble yourself and ask forgiveness. If you can resolve the difference by a personal meeting, by all means do it.

One pastor with an opposing board member sensed trouble for months, but he refused to take the man out for lunch because he feared direct confrontation. His refusal only increased the alienation. Finally, reconciliation became impossible.

All disagreements aren't necessarily bad or the evidence of carnality. Remember that Barnabas wanted to take Mark on the second missionary journey, but Paul disagreed, reminding him that the young man had deserted them in Pamphylia. Luke wrote, "And there arose such a sharp disagreement that they separated from one another, and Barnabas took Mark with him and sailed away to Cyprus" (Acts 15:39).

Sometimes there is no easy answer to who is right or wrong. If possible, work out a solution to accommodate the critic's legitimate complaints. Maybe you could change the order of worship from time to time or begin to teach that Bible class. Many a potential troublemaker has been diffused by reasonable compromise.

But there are some critics (Shelley calls them "dragons") who will never be satisfied. They criticize because of personal problems that defy resolution. It is like the story of the drunkard who'd had strong smelling cheese smeared on his mustache before he left the saloon. As the man staggered into the clear night air he muttered, "The whole world stinks!"

With such a person, you must make a choice. Ask yourself, *How deeply do I feel about this matter? Can I live with the situation, accepting it from God as His means of personal refinement?* Spurgeon said, "Get a friend to tell you your faults, or better still, welcome an enemy who will watch you keenly and sting you savagely. What a blessing such an irritating critic will be to a wise man, what an intolerable nuisance to a fool!" (cited in *Well-Intentioned Dragons*, p. 107).

Taking a stand. But perhaps you think the matter is important enough to put your reputation on the line. If there appears to be no resolution and if the disagreement interferes with your ability to minister, then you must throw the matter into the lap of the board and be prepared to accept the consequences.

Scripture teaches that those who walk disorderly should be disciplined. Paul also wrote, "And if anyone does not obey our instruction in this letter, take special note of that man and do not associate with him, so that he may be put to shame. And yet do not regard him as an enemy, but admonish him as a brother" (2 Thessalonians 3:14-15).

If the board decisively backs you and admonishes those who sow discord, you can continue your ministry with confidence. If you have built solid relationships with board members, they will be prepared to give your viewpoint due consideration. But if the board thinks the criticism is justified or if the men are too weak to stand against those who would polarize the church, you may have no recourse but to resign.

Unfortunately, board members tend to side with those who've been their friends in the church for many years. It's particularly difficult when the troublemaker is married to the choir leader or is related to four other families in the congregation.

In one church, the entire board opposed the pastor because of the persuasive power of one woman who had indirectly controlled the church for years. In a vendetta against the pastor, she even suggested that he should divorce his wife, though they had been happily married for thirty-eight years! Yet board members were so mesmerized by her that they accepted her criticisms, and the pastor was forced to resign.

In such situations, a pastor can either carry his hurts with him and poison his future usefulness to God or come to terms with the injustice. This particular pastor committed the matter to the Lord, believing that God would ultimately untangle the mess at the judgment seat. He has been blessed in special ways and will undoubtedly be used of God in the future.

Peter Marshall said, "It is a fact of Christian experience that life is a series of troughs and peaks. In His efforts to get permanent possession of the soul, God relies on the troughs more than the peaks. And some of His special favorites have gone through longer and deeper troughs than anyone else" (cited in *Well-Intentioned Dragons*, p. 133).

When we encounter dragons, remember that if they are believers, they too are loved by God. He can use us in their lives, but He can also use them in ours. There is no one answer to all situations. But Shelley does state one cardinal rule: *When attacked by a dragon, do not become one.*

As my friend said, God will have to untangle many things at the judgment seat. Sometimes it's best we leave it to Him rather than try to do it ourselves.

Nothing like "Soul to Soul"
to stir the heart.

5

Preaching:
How Can We Reach Their Souls?

Charles Spurgeon once walked into a new auditorium and tested the acoustics by shouting, "Behold the Lamb of God, which taketh away the sin of the world." A workman who overheard him was smitten with conviction and was converted.

Some preachers get a better response than others. If ten pastors preached the same message verbatim, the results would not be the same. Some exude instant charisma, others are more yielded to the Spirit or have greater gifts. It's not just what is said but who says it that makes the difference.

Sermons with good content may fall flat for many reasons. Perhaps the most common is that they are delivered with an absence of feeling.

We've all fallen into the rut of preaching unfelt truth. We've rattled through a message as if it were a stock market report at the end of a lackluster day of trading. Vance Havner said, "I've never heard a sermon from which I didn't get something, but I've had some mighty close calls."

When I was a teenager, I wondered why the pastor didn't simply mimeograph his messages and mail them. That would have enabled us to get the truth without the effort of going to church. Now I wonder if I entertained such thoughts because the pastor preached so nonchalantly that his personal delivery added nothing to the message.

Preaching is not just giving a message. "Preaching is the art of making a sermon and delivering it?" asked Bishop William A. Quayle. "Why no, that's not preaching. Preaching is the art of making a preacher and delivering that!"

It's the preacher's delivering himself that is absent from so many of our pulpits on Sunday mornings. Many who preach have no fire in their bones.

Michael Tucker, a pastor in Colorado, writes of an effective preacher: "Preaching must pump his heart until he lives and breathes the message. The message will hound him, drive him, even explode within him. So great will be the desire to preach that he will find it difficult to wait for the time to deliver the message of God."

George Whitefield preached with intensity. He wrote to a friend, "Speak every time as if it was your last. Weep out, if possible, every argument, and as it were, compel them to cry, 'Behold how he loveth us!'"

Jesuit theologian Walter Burghardt deplores the perfunctory remarks made by priests in their homilies. He laments that the laity of the Roman Catholic church is "puzzled by our ability to declaim about the divine without a shred of feeling or emotion." His words apply to many evangelical ministers, too.

Three styles of preaching. Richard Owen Roberts, author of the book *Revival*, speaks of three levels of sermon preparation. The first is mouth-to-ear preaching. That's when a man is greatly concerned about the choice and organization of his words. He's conscious of the need for good illustrations and vivid descriptions. He's careful to work on key phrases and unique expressions. A typical listener responds, "What a lovely sermon. I really enjoyed it!"

Then there is head-to-head preaching. It stimulates thought and challenges the minds of the listeners. The preacher aims at being well organized, theologically accurate, and enlightening. At the door he hears, "That was a great sermon. I never thought of that before."

In soul-to-soul preaching, the preacher spends hours preparing his message but equal time preparing his soul. Only that kind of preaching results in conversions and personal holiness.

That explains why some of the most effective preachers are not the most eloquent. Some who have ordinary gifts are used in extraordinary ways because they deliver not only a message but also themselves. Quite literally they become the message they are preaching.

Three persons of preaching. How can we preach in such a way that we stir the emotions and move the will? Shouting won't do it, nor will dramatic stories. We must become intimately aware of the three personalities involved in the preaching event.

The first is God. Peter wrote, "Whoever speaks, let him speak, as it were, the utterances of God" (1 Peter 4:11). A preacher speaks on God's behalf; if the sermon is boring, repetitious, or perfunctory, that's the way the congregation will perceive God's message.

Does God have a relevant word for today? Has He spoken with clarity about the issues that face the members of our congregations? Can He demolish walls of hatred and suspicion among families and believers? All of these and a hundred other questions are being answered when we speak on His behalf.

We can't represent Him effectively unless we spend time meditating on His attributes. We must stand in awe of His holiness as displayed in that thunderous revelation at Mount Sinai, of His sovereignty in creation and history, of His love as shown at the cross.

"For thus says the high and exalted One who lives forever, whose name is holy, 'I dwell on a high and holy place, and also with the contrite and lowly of spirit in order to revive the spirit of the lowly and to revive the heart of the contrite'" (Isaiah 57:15).

The first step in rekindling our emotional fires in preaching is to grasp anew the wonder of our privilege as messengers of the Most High. We must know Him well before we can effectively represent Him to others.

The second person involved in the sermon is the listener. Let's discard the idea that if we talk others will listen. People do not come to church with open minds.

Haddon Robinson, president of Conservative Baptist Theological Seminary in Denver, says, "Heads are neither open nor hollow. Heads have lids, screwed on tightly, and no amount of pouring can force ideas inside. Minds open only when their owners sense a need to open them. Even then, ideas must still filter through layers of experience, habit, prejudice, fear, and suspicion."

Anger, for example, may prevent a person from listening. A parishioner's teenage son fell asleep at the wheel of his car and was killed. The insensitive pastor said to the distraught father, "Don't expect me to take the funeral, because I'm going on vacation."

The father told me later, "Even though he was a good preacher, after that remark I never heard a word he said in his sermons."

That illustrates an important principle of communication: you can preach up a storm, but if a person is not disposed to listen, it penetrates no farther than water on a marble slab.

Or maybe the parishioner is thinking about the pressures of the past week, family problems, or financial reversals. Add to that the depravity of the natural mind and Satan's ability to snatch the Word of God from people's hearts, and it's a miracle that communication takes place at all.

We can't pry through this grid unless we genuinely love our people and bear their needs close to our hearts. Information alone will not change their attitudes and behavior. They must see us bleed along with them. We must enter into the hurts of their world.

Finally, there is the preacher. He must apply the truth to himself before he shares it with others. That is difficult for those of us who preach two or three times per week. But we cannot afford to pass on truths that are supposed to work but haven't worked for us. We must share ourselves so that people can see we are a part of the message we are bringing.

Expressing honest feelings isn't easy. Bombarded with human need, we insulate ourselves from the emotional overload we encounter day by day. We are unable to weep for those in need as Christ did when He stood on the Mount of Olives and wept for Jerusalem. Seminary has trained us to think deeply but not to feel deeply.

Our preaching's effectiveness would rise dramatically if we followed a simple rule: let's not preach beyond our experience. When we share the message God has given us, we should know it well enough that we can concentrate on its content rather than worry about remembering its outline. Only then can we say with authority, "Thus says the Lord."

Perhaps we ought to follow John Owen, a Puritan scholar and pastor of the seventeenth century, in taking a vow before we step into the pulpit: "I therefore hold myself bound in conscience and in honor, not even to imagine that I have attained a proper knowledge of any one article of truth, much less to publish it, unless through the Holy Spirit I have had such a taste of it, in its spiritual sense, that I may be able from the heart to say with the psalmist, 'I have believed and therefore have spoken'" (*Sin and Temptation* [Portland, Oreg.: Multnomah, 1983], p. xviii).

If we spend as much time preparing our hearts as we do our minds, our congregations will know that they have heard from God.

I need one that is quite
a bit smaller, has an odd
shape and a dull finish.

6
Christian Loafers:
Can We Get Them in Step?

Faithfulness. You've preached on it; so have I. But have our sermons done much good? At a recent pastors' conference, several men shared with me their frustration about the casual attitude some believers have in serving the church. Every congregation can boast of a few dependable, joyful volunteers. Unfortunately, they are sometimes the exception rather than the rule.

The casually committed are those who arrive habitually late to every meeting. Some must even plan to be late. I'm sure they haven't heard the invocation of a morning service for years.

Then there are those who never let anyone know when they will be absent. Sunday school teachers, ushers, and committee workers simply don't show up for their assigned responsibilities. Consequently, someone has to scurry around looking for a harried replacement.

We're all acquainted with those who accept responsibilities but don't follow through. Jane promises to offer Donna a ride; John will see if Bill needs further counsel; Peter vows to write an important letter; Frank assures you he will be at the next committee meeting. But nothing happens—not this week or the next five.

Our congregations are also populated with those who justify their negligence with flimsy excuses. "We had company," someone will say. "The weather turned cold" (or hot or windy or humid, depending on your location).

Such performances would not be tolerated in the secular world. Many believers who would never be late on Monday morning shirk their Sunday duties without a twinge of conscience. Of course, we can't threaten to fire them.

An army of volunteers. "Remember, these are all volunteers," someone once said to me. "You can't fire people who don't get paid. When you've got a volunteer army, you take what you can get."

So we continue with latecomers, promise-breakers, and procrastinators. And our volunteer army limps along. Many of us can appreciate this parody of the hymn "Onward Christian Soldiers":

> Like a mighty turtle,
> Moves the church of God;
> Brothers, we are treading
> Where we've always trod.

In a recent *Atlantic Monthly* article, James Fallows bemoans the deterioration of the U.S. Army since the draft was abandoned. He quotes an essay published in 1980 by William Hauser, a retired colonel.

Hauser claims there are four elements sustaining the "will to fight." To learn *submission*, a soldier must repeat disagreeable tasks. To counter *fear*, he must know and trust his comrades. That will encourage him to fight alongside them instead of running from the enemy.

To evoke *loyalty*, the Army requires the men to sleep, work, and eat together. They will eventually gain a sense of responsibility for one another's welfare. Finally, *pride* reminds a man that others depend on him and value his contribution to the unit's safety and success.

Each of those qualities, however, has diminished with the volunteer force. Recruitment is now based largely on self-interest rather than service to our nation. As a result, those who enlist are only casually committed.

Sound familiar? I think it's time we challenged the notion that the church is a volunteer army. Since when did God give us the option of enlisting? Does He discuss terms of commitment with us? Should faithfulness be expected only of those who get paid for their work?

An army under orders. Let's remind ourselves of some facts. First, we didn't choose Christ; He chose us. Jesus said, "You did not choose Me, but I chose you, and appointed you, that you should go and bear fruit" (John 15:16). As Commander-in-Chief, He has a role for each of us to play. We are, as Peter Marshall pointed out, "sealed under orders."

Our Commander decides how and where the battles should be fought. Paul learned submission and obedience by becoming Christ's bondslave. We can't ignore the divine call, either, without becoming an outright deserter.

Second, faithfulness in small details promotes greater responsibility. "He who is faithful in a very little thing is faithful also in much; and he who is unrighteous in a very little thing is unrighteous also in much" (Luke 16:10).

As pastors, we wouldn't think of being late for a morning worship service—after all, it's a public event. But is it any less important to be on time for Sunday school or a counseling appointment? In the eyes of men, yes; in the eyes of God, no.

When it comes to seeking obedience from their children, parents care little whether they are working on minor or major tasks. It's the child's attitude of obedience that counts. Our heavenly Father shares the same sentiments. When we are unfaithful in so-called small matters, we insult our Commander-in-Chief. He doesn't overlook apparently insignificant details. Even a cup of cold water offered in Christ's name merits reward.

Third, our motivation must be to please the Lord, not men. Paul wrote to Timothy, "No soldier in active service entangles himself in the affairs of everyday life, so that he may please the one who enlisted him as a soldier" (2 Timothy 2:4).

In Napoleon's army, men endured physical pain, illness, or even the sacrifice of an arm or leg just for an approving nod. Nothing will purify our motives like deciding to be obedient to Jesus, whether or not we are recognized in this world.

When washing the disciples' feet or preaching the Sermon on the Mount, Christ had the same motivation. He said, "I always do the things that are pleasing to [My Father]" (John 8:29). He wasn't playing the game of life for the benefit of His contemporaries. He did not consider Himself merely a volunteer but a humble servant compelled to do the Father's will.

Even the ungodly are faithful when they're getting paid. Christians, however, should be distinguished by their positive attitudes toward minor, unrewarded tasks.

How can we, like Gideon, distinguish between the committed worker and the one along for the ride? We might want to grant an honorable discharge to anyone within the church shirking his or her responsibilities. It is better, though, for people to recognize their own deficiencies and dismiss themselves from active service.

Begin by establishing written performance standards for church positions. Those could include attendance, follow-through in responsibilities, and an outline of acceptable performance. Then share the guidelines with committee and board members. Let it be known that church leaders expect faithfulness.

Don't be afraid to let someone go. If you need to, leave a position vacant. That is a better option than filling it with another nonperformer. Look and wait for a qualified, reliable replacement.

Pastors, we need to display faithfulness in our own responsibilities. God will eventually provide a core of dedicated soldiers, willing to endure hardship for the cause of Christ. Increasing the number of dependable, qualified, and deeply committed believers starts with us.

A volunteer army will never do. Only one conscripted by a higher calling will have the determination to finish the task.

7
Church Splits:
When Are They Worth the Cost?

I'm weary of hearing about church splits over trivial issues.

In one church, a few men wanted their pastor to enforce a dress code and to conduct the services according to their liking. He didn't fully accommodate them. Because they thought their authority was slighted, small matters were magnified.

Soon everything the pastor did was wrong. His detractors scrutinized his sermons to find hidden meanings directed toward them.

That pastor resigned. He probably had the support of 90 percent of the congregation, but he grew tired of the hassle. He was not a fighter. He left an effective ministry because of a few disgruntled members.

How long has it been since you heard that a church was divided because of the virgin birth or salvation by faith in Christ alone? Most of the strife I hear about concerns budgets, music, or leadership philosophy. Often, the real issue is who's in charge.

My friend's resignation caused me to reflect on this question: What should a church member do if he or she wants to voice a legitimate complaint? Most of the people are not on a church board, yet they have deep feelings about the ministry of the church.

What usually happens? Unfortunately, many church members take one of two courses of action. The first is to share criticism with others in order to drum up support.

The tongue is the greatest cause for division within the church. "And the tongue is a fire, the very world of iniquity; the tongue is set among our members as that which defiles the entire body, and sets on fire the course of our life, and is set on fire by hell" (James 3:6).

To use our tongues to rally support for our viewpoints is to spread the fires of hell within the church. Sometimes the church is already polarized over an issue before the elders or pastor even know about the problem.

An equally disastrous procedure is to bring up the matter in a church business meeting. Often, that is done to score points publicly even when no attempt has been made to resolve the issue privately. Any matter that can be dealt with between one or two members or that could be cared for through other legitimate channels should never be mentioned for public discussion.

I know a pastor who was humiliated in a church business meeting; he had to endure totally unexpected personal criticisms. Surely Satan must rejoice in church meetings where everyone feels he has the freedom to air his favorite gripe.

We must instruct our congregations on the need for unity, but at the same time we should allow for dialogue regarding disagreements. If not, resentment and misunderstanding will only build.

What can be done? First, we ourselves must set an example of submission. Paul wrote, "Be subject to one another in the fear of Christ" (Ephesians 5:21).

I wince when I hear a pastor teach his congregation to submit to authority when he believes he is an exception to the rule. "I'm accountable to God alone" sounds pious, but it can be poisonous.

The New Testament teaches that a congregation is to have a plurality of godly leaders with no one person assuming the role of dictator. Though some congregations are polite enough to tolerate authoritarianism, others chafe under the strain. Individuals know that their input is worthless because the pastor receives his instruction privately from God.

Don't be surprised, then, when believers feel frustrated in their attempts to get their points across. If the pastor is a law unto himself, why cannot they be? Like pastor, like people.

No doubt many churches have split because God wanted to bring the pastor and the congregation to a place of mutual submission. But when the pastor isn't responsive to the authority of his board, the congregation often rejects the authority of the pastor as well. Meanwhile, the gap between the pastor and the board widens.

Second, we must teach that Matthew 18:15-16 applies to all kinds of disagreements. "And if your brother sins, go and reprove him in private; if he listens to you, you have won your brother. But if he does not listen to you, take one or two more with you, so that by the mouth of two or three witnesses every fact may be confirmed."

The believer is responsible to go directly to the person against whom he has a grievance. If the issue involves specific sin, then there is an obligation to go to the person even if he is a church leader. But Paul warned, "Do not receive an accusation against an elder except on the basis of two or three witnesses" (1 Timothy 5:19).

If the issue remains unresolved, then others, particularly other members of the church board, must become involved. And the elder or pastor must defer to their authority.

But what about opposition to a building program, the pastor's salary, or the length of his sermons? To discuss such disagreements with members of the congregation sows seeds of discord that grieve the heart of God. Here also, members should go directly to the person responsible even if it means a trip to the pastor's office or writing him a signed letter.

At this point our attitude as pastor is critical. If we ignore what is said or if we dismiss the criticism without learning from it, we may be encouraging the concerned member to try another approach—to recruit other members to his position through gossip.

I've found that an honest discussion clears the air and can cement a relationship even if the disagreement persists. There's something gratifying about having someone else earnestly try to see your point of view even if he remains unconvinced.

That doesn't mean we have to take all the suggestions given to us. But I've often found that there may be more truth to criticism than we are willing to admit. It's easy to listen politely but then dismiss what has been said without thoughtful consideration and prayer.

In my opinion, that is as far as a church member is allowed to go in pursuing a point of disagreement. Of course, I don't mean to stifle profitable discussion among church members about improving the ministry or talking about matters in preparation for a church business meeting. We should expect our people to discuss various ministries within the church. But once a decision is made, there must be submission to the will of those in authority.

In a day when people demand their rights, it's difficult for a congregation to submit to church leaders and wait for God to work His will even in controversial decisions. Sometimes a member of the congregation might have an idea that is correct, but the timing is wrong. We forget that God works among His people despite diversity of opinion and imperfections of church leaders.

That holds for those of us who are on a church board as well. I've had to submit to the will of leaders even on those occasions when I may have had a difference of opinion. God is honored when we are willing to set aside disagreements over nonbiblical issues for the unity and harmony of the Body.

Only heaven will reveal the damage done to the Body of Christ by members of the congregation who feel called to correct all the faults of the church or to campaign for their pet grievances.

I fear for those who are determined to force the resignation of a man of God by petty criticisms. I fear for those who have divided a congregation because of intransigence over a building program or the proposed budget.

Yes, there are times when a church split is justified, perhaps even necessary. But let's be sure that it's over a clear biblical issue and not just a preference we hold dearly.

Paul wrote, "If any man destroys the temple of God, God will destroy him, for the temple of God is holy, and that is what you are" (1 Corinthians 3:17). The word *temple* refers to the congregation of believers.

God says He will destroy the one who destroys the work of the church. Often, He grants that person a hard and bitter heart, or He may use other means of discipline.

Dr. Paul Brand says that white blood cells, the armed forces of the body, guard against invaders. When the body's been cut, these cells abruptly stop their aimless wandering and home in from all different directions on the scene of the battle.

As if they have a sense of smell, they hurry through tissue via the most direct route. When they arrive, many give their lives to kill the bacteria. They subject themselves to the good of the larger organism that determines their duties.

If a cell should lose its loyalty and cling to its own life, it shares the benefits of the body but sets up a rival organism called cancer.

Our churches are filled with parasites who benefit from the ministry but who refuse to submit themselves to the leader of the organism. As a result, the body is cancerous, weak, and unprepared for battle. Sometimes so much energy is spent in resolving internal conflict that there is no time to confront the world with Jesus Christ.

If we're guilty of dividing the Body, we'd better repent. When we disagree with church leaders, we should talk to God rather than our friends.

He is able to direct His own church in His own time and in His own way. To destroy the temple of God is to toy with the wrath of God.

8
Politics:
Where Should We Draw the Line?

Some fundamentalist preachers have jumped into the political arena with both feet, causing pastors to rethink their stand on political involvement.

There are good arguments in favor of political activism. Americans are entitled to work through the political process to effect change. Why should evangelicals sell out to radical feminists, gay liberationists, and abortionists? We have an agenda of our own and a right to be heard. Perhaps the ballot box does speak louder than words.

What better way to get our message across than to organize and vote the humanists out of office? Why not elect those who would enact laws that reflect a more biblical approach to morality? In a democracy, political power talks.

Then there is the precedence set by liberal religious organizations such as the World Council of Churches, which uses political clout to accomplish social and economic change.

Fundamentalism, often ridiculed as an embarrassing anachronism in American history, has finally tasted political power.

I agree that we can be grateful for every Christian in politics; we ought to support organizations that attempt to educate the religious constituency of the issues being debated in Washington. Christians ought to make their influence felt in local as well as national elections and speak up for what they believe. Often, we've lost crucial battles by default.

But what role should ministers play in all of this?

Jerry Falwell has skillfully united Christians, Jews, Mormons, and anyone else who is willing to support a return to a conservative political and moral perspective. This political force had a significant impact in the 1980 election.

Yet I am troubled when I see ministers speak out on matters that would be better left to politicians. I'm also troubled when I hear them endorse a particular party or candidate. Speaking as a private citizen is one thing, but to use the pulpit as a platform for political endorsement is another.

The dangers of political involvement. The first danger is that biblical and political issues tend to be mixed together as part of one lump.

Abortion is a biblical issue—we can all unite in opposition to the arbitrary killing of human life. But what about the need for a stronger defense—the MX missile, for example? Even if I favor a strong military, should I play the part of the expert and go on record about how big our defense budget should be?

We as ministers dare not give the impression that our armaments will keep us from falling into the hands of the Soviets. We of all people should know what may have escaped the attention of the Pentagon: regardless of its military might, any nation will fall when God appoints that its time has come.

The city of Babylon was justifiably considered impregnable. It was captured not because it lacked solid defenses but because God weighed it on His scale and found righteousness wanting.

Certainly God may use our ICBMs to deter the Russians. But I'd feel safer with fewer defense systems and a national revival than with the proposed Dense Pack and spiritual indifference.

Suppose we achieved substantial superiority over the Russians. That could give us a false sense of security; we'd be tempted to have misplaced faith in weapons rather than in God.

Let our defense experts decide how many bombs we need. Our message as ministers must be clear: repent, or judgment of some kind is inevitable, a huge defense budget notwithstanding.

Second, I fear that political reformation could subtly substitute for spiritual transformation. Of course we all favor laws that reflect biblical morality. But even such progress falls far short of the real answer to our national decay.

Suppose prayer is restored in the public schools. In our society, such prayer would be based on the lowest common denominator of all religions. Christ's name would not be mentioned, hardly a credit to the One whose sacrifice is the only means of reconciling our nation to God.

Suppose it were mandatory to teach creationism in our public schools. That would hardly make us a Christian nation. Whatever lip service we could achieve through such laws would fall short of the change of heart God desires.

Civil religion can help bring about a moral reformation. But at the same time, it gives a false sense of security. We may honor God with our lips, but our hearts are far from Him. We know that law cannot save an individual; it cannot save a country either. As ministers we must never settle for less than the radical transformation of heart God requires.

Third, what if we simply don't have the political power to bring about reform? And when we openly join with those who explicitly deny the gospel in our effort to turn America back to God, are we not thereby leaning on a broken reed?

Yes, we might win some battles, make a few reforms. But our gains are dependent on the ballot box. In a democratic political process, one reaction will always spawn another. Someone once said that "the art of politics is the art of destroying your enemies." To fight moral issues with political muscle is a high-risk venture that fluctuates each passing year.

Christ was largely silent about political matters. He never encouraged a revolution against Rome.

Paul did not speak out against slavery lest Christianity be charged with causing political upheaval. Instead he taught slaves to "regard their own masters as worthy of all honor so that the name of God and our doctrine may not be spoken against" (1 Timothy 6:1). He did not want to identify with external political and social change that might detract from the purity of the gospel.

Our response. What should our response be in the face of the moral and spiritual decline of our nation?

First, we must admit that the true church is defenseless in the world. We are strangers and pilgrims who cannot afford to pin our hope on the fortunes of the erratic political process. God alone is our defender.

Fortunately, our strength does not depend on a political majority. The fortunes of a nation often depend on a godly minority, as in the case of Gideon. If God does not take up our cause and fight in our behalf, we shall eventually be destroyed.

Second, we must understand the exalted role the church plays in the political affairs of this world. The bride of Christ holds back the coming judgment of God. The church is number one on God's agenda. Everything He does in this world is somehow related to the Body of Christ, and thus everything shall someday be summed up in Him (Ephesians 1:10).

Therefore, our spiritual condition as a church determines in a large measure God's blessing or judgment on our nation. Too often we have blamed the humanists for the moral decay around us without realizing that God may be judging us through them. It was God's prophet Jonah, not the pagan sailors, who caused the storm on the Mediterranean.

If we are able to turn our nation back to God, it most likely should be attributed to a godly remnant's intercessory prayer for spiritual revival. The righteousness that exalts a nation is the fruit of repentance.

Finally, as ministers we must address the moral issues of our time with courage and clarity. Our position on abortion and homosexual perspectives must be knowledgeably analyzed and critiqued. Whenever the laws of the state conflict with clear biblical convictions, we must obey God rather than men even if it means going to jail.

We must not be intimidated by those who wish to silence the mouths of ministers under the guise of separation of church and state. But we must also remember that our message is not a political agenda but the full biblical mandate of submission to the will of God.

To fulfill such a calling we cannot be publicly wedded to any political party. Of course we vote, but we don't tell our congregation how they should. In our fallen world, even born-again candidates can disappoint us. Each party has its own peculiar blend of good and evil. We must condemn evil wherever it is found without any indebtedness to a party or candidate.

The revivals of John Wesley and George Whitefield resulted in great social changes. God brought that about by the miracle of the new birth. He prefers to work from the inside out. What political power could never do, the conviction and the power of the Holy Spirit accomplished.

I believe it's time for us as individuals and churches to seek the Lord with repentant hearts. If we look to Washington, we will often be disappointed. We cannot depend on political power. We can only submit ourselves unreservedly to the will of God and become personal and corporate witnesses to His power in our decadent society.

If our problems were political, a political solution would be all that was needed. But if they are spiritual, they must be addressed from that vantage point.

If we as God's people repent, He may yet restore the years that the locusts have eaten. For in God we have the greatest power that could ever be unleashed. Politics is the art of achieving the possible, but faith is the art of achieving the impossible.

This nation needs to experience the impossible.

9

Envy: How Can We Live
in the Shadow of Success?

There is a fable that Satan's emissaries were trying to tempt a holy man who lived in the Libyan desert. Try as they might, the demons could not get the man to sin. The seductions of the flesh and the onslaught of doubts and fears left him unmoved.

Angered by their failure, Satan stepped forward. "Your methods are too crude," he said. "Just watch." He whispered in the holy man's ear, "Your brother has just been made Bishop of Alexandria."

Instantly a malignant scowl clouded the holy man's face. "Envy," Satan said to his cohorts, "is our final weapon for those who seek holiness."

Making comparisons. As pastors, we struggle with the same enticements as do the people in our congregations. But because our ministries are public, our most powerful temptation may be envy. We all know how much it hurts to be compared with a pastor who is more successful.

"You're OK, but you're no Swindoll," a parishioner tells us with a touch of finality. Or a board member asks, "Why aren't we growing like Jerry Falwell's congregation?"

But such comments are passing, and we can handle them with a bit of good humor. It's more difficult when your congregation prefers your assistant pastor's preaching—or when the church next door is bursting at the seams while yours is slowly declining.

Then it's easy to become critical and defensive. We say we have "a ministry depth, not a numbers racket." Or we accuse the congregation of liking the assistant's preaching better because he "tickles their ears."

Our fallen nature loathes to be cast in bad light. It's difficult to rejoice with those who are more successful. At times we even take a quiet satisfaction when we learn about others' failures; by comparison we are doing better.

What aggravates the problem is that God's blessings seem so inconsistent. We see a church with phenomenal growth even though its pastor is a dull preacher who does little to inspire his congregation. At the same time, another church with an excellent preacher with good public relations skills may decline in membership.

There are pastors whose theology is weak, whose methods of fund-raising are suspect, and whose personal lives are in shambles, yet they are blessed with growth and money. Meanwhile, there are pastors who have integrity and faithfully teach the Word of God, yet they can't raise enough money to paint the church. No wonder a missionary once said to me, "Have you ever noticed how often God puts His hand on the wrong person?"

Ministry erosion. Envy will cripple any pastor and his ministry. First, it erodes faith. Jesus asked the Pharisees, who were men pleasers, "How can you believe, when you receive glory from one another, and you do not seek the glory that is from the one and only God?" (John 5:44). With their eyes on one another, they were unable to focus their eyes on God. The envious are in no position to please God. They are not free to believe wholeheartedly in Christ.

Second, envy produces isolationism. A pastor who fears the success of others will withdraw from fellowship and cooperation with other churches. He may say his reason for separation is the need for doctrinal purity. At times, important doctrinal matters are at stake and separatism is necessary. But if our hidden motives were exposed, much of our separation is rooted in the fear of allowing our congregations to be blessed outside the walls of our own little kingdom.

Although the Pharisees gave the excuse of doctrinal reasons, that was not the real reason they condemned Christ. Pilate discerned their underlying motive: "For he knew that because of envy they had delivered Him up" (Matthew 27:18). Envy was the motive; theology was the smoke screen.

Paul had a similar experience in Pisidian Antioch where his preaching drew large crowds. "But when the Jews saw the crowds, they were filled with jealousy, and began contradicting the things spoken by Paul, and were blaspheming" (Acts 13:45). Once again theology was the excuse for antagonism, but the motivation was less noble.

Writing to the Philippians, Paul discerned that some were preaching Christ out of envy and strife, hoping to make him look bad. Yet he rejoiced that Christ was preached, even though their motives were sinful (1:12-18).

An envious person may fear unfavorable comparison so much that he works behind the scenes to sabotage a colleague's ministry. Done carefully, his hidden motive may never come to light.

Saul was not as careful in his attempt to hide his jealousy. He was so angered by the comparison in the cheers of the crowd, "Saul has slain his thousands, and David his ten thousands," that he became obsessed with killing his young rival (1 Samuel 18:7). God's response was to send a demon to trouble Saul, evidently so he would be goaded into repentance. But Saul eventually committed suicide instead. Once envy has found a home in the human heart, it resists eviction. Even death may seem more attractive than conceding success to someone who is younger and less qualified.

Defeating envy. How do we overcome this deceitful monster? We must treat envy for the sin it is. It is rebellion against God's providential leading in the lives of His children. An envious person is saying God has no right to bless someone else more than himself.

Jesus told a parable about a landowner who agreed to pay a denarius a day to workers who arrived early. Others who came later in the day didn't haggle about their wages but were willing to trust the landowner's fairness.

At the end of the day, those who came last were the first to be paid. Each received a denarius. Those who'd worked since morning assumed they'd be paid more but were shocked to receive one denarius also (Matthew 20:1-12).

It seems unfair. Imagine an employer paying those who arrive at 3:00 P.M. the same as those who show up on time. But Jesus gave the story a twist: it was fair because the first workers got what they'd agreed on. If the landowner wanted to pay the latecomers that much, too, he was at liberty to do so.

Speaking for the landowner, who represents God, Jesus said, "Is it not lawful for me to do what I wish with what is my own? Or is your eye envious because I am generous?'" (v. 15).

God can do what He wishes with His own. He can be more generous with others, and we have no right to complain. Envy is rebellion against His sovereign rights.

Envy is also a sin against God's goodness. Whatever we have, be it little or much, it is a gift of God. When Jesus Christ eclipsed his ministry, and he was tempted to envy, John the Baptist rightly replied, "A man can receive nothing, unless it has been given him from heaven" (John 3:27). Envy is based on the assumption that our abilities and gifts are something we're entitled to have.

Envy is a sin that lashes out against God's goodness and sovereignty. It's the pot telling the potter how to make other vessels. Francis Schaeffer said there is no such thing as small people and big people, only consecrated people and unconsecrated people. One pastor said, "When I finally accepted the fact that God did not want me to be well-known, I began to experience His blessing."

All comparison of one ministry or one person with another is sinful. We can easily see that a skyscraper is taller than a small apartment building, but if we compare both buildings against the height of a distant star, there's not much difference between them. Likewise, the differences among us fade into oblivion when we compare ourselves with Christ.

God wants to give us humble satisfaction with our place in His vineyard. Having any place in the vineyard affirms His mercy and grace. To envy those who are given greater blessing is to imbibe a spirit of thanklessness and rebellion.

Moses was a Spirit-filled man, but God multiplied his ministry in the lives of seventy elders who were given the gift of prophecy. Two of those elders, Eldad and Medad, were particularly gifted and prophesied in the camp. When a young man came running to Moses and told him the news, Joshua said to Moses, "My lord, restrain them." But Moses answered, "Are you jealous for my sake? Would that all the Lord's people were prophets, that the Lord would put His Spirit upon them" (Numbers 11:28-29).

You can't destroy a man who rejoices in the success of others. He has a proper perspective about himself and his God. He can rejoice in those who are more successful. He's thankful for even the small opportunities to serve, because he hasn't lost the wonder of the Father's care. And a genuine smile breaks forth when you tell him that his brother has been appointed Bishop of Alexandria.

10

Burnout:
Can Wet Wood Still Be Ignited?

A church janitor was heard to say, "The blower still works, but the fire has gone out." He was discussing a problem with the furnace, but the parishioner who overheard him thought he was speaking about the pastor.

One definition of *burnout* is "a syndrome of emotional exhaustion, depersonalization, and reduced personal accomplishment that can occur among individuals who do 'people work' of some kind." Its symptoms include increased fatigue; feeling tired even after a good night's sleep; losing interest in your work; and a pessimistic, critical spirit often accompanied by withdrawal, depression, and a feeling of futility.

Burnout, however, may be beneficial as a warning that something has gone wrong, according to Archibald D. Hart, dean of the graduate school of psychology at Fuller Theological Seminary. It may intervene and take you out of a harmful environment when you're on the road to stressful destruction. "It instantly slows you down and produces a state of lethargy and disengagement," Hart says. "The system 'gives out' before it 'blows up.'"

Whereas stress is characterized by over-involvement, burnout is characterized by withdrawal, a loss of meaning and hope. Regardless of what the person does, the rewards seem too small to bother.

Causes of burnout. One study indicated that one-third of the pastors surveyed had considered leaving the ministry because of burnout. Although it can occur in all professions, ministers are particularly vulnerable. One reason may be the conflict of roles.

We are expected to be good preachers, counselors, and organizers; know something about publicity; and have the fine art of loving people and showing it in our relationships. When not accompanied by rewards, the pushes and pulls of those expectations can lead to a sense of futility and despair. Because people come to the pastor to get rather than give, his emotional resources can easily become depleted.

Second, the pastor is often alone in his struggles. Though the members of the church can speak freely to him about their problems, he is not free to reciprocate. As J. Grant Swank, Jr., says, "Pastors wonder who is going to pull the supports out from under them if they open up, if they are honest about the tensions of the pastorate. Consequently, in too many cases it is very hard for the minister to discover a partner in ministry other than the spouse" ("Who Counsels Pastors When They Have Problems?" *Christianity Today,* 25 November 1983, p. 58).

If the pastor's marriage is falling apart or if his children are an embarrassment, he feels trapped and unable to extricate himself from his emotional lows. Soon he wonders how he can be of help to others when he himself has such a strong sense of failure.

All of us have feelings of inadequacy. And we are not helped when we are compared with the television preachers who are able to draw large crowds and money. Though our faults are well-known to our congregations, the people hear only of the successes of radio and television preachers.

If we preach one poor sermon, everyone knows it; if we get indignant at a board meeting, word gets around. Soon we think we are unappreciated. If we are particularly sensitive to criticism, we will try to overachieve to please everyone. If we don't receive adequate emotional and spiritual compensation for our efforts, we will be left wondering if it's all worthwhile.

Dr. David Congo, associated with H. Norman Wright's Family Counseling Clinic in Santa Ana, California, says the ministry can be represented by either a "rat race" or a "relay race." Both require a great deal of energy, but in a rat race there is no clear sense of purpose. In a relay race, however, there is direction and a prescribed course, along with cooperation and team spirit. The pastor in a rat race often feels like a victim controlled by his situation. It's hard to say whether that is the cause of burnout or its result, but in either case there's a direct relationship.

Congo goes on to list four personality types linked to burnout: (1) those with a high need for approval, (2) the workaholic, (3) the unassertive, passive victim, and (4) those with a "messiah complex" *(Theology News and Notes,* March 1984, p. 8).

All of us are tempted to give beyond our own spiritual and emotional resources to be thought of as successful. That may result in a feeling of fulfillment. Or it may do the opposite—lead to inner anger and disillusionment.

If a pastor feels unappreciated, his response may be to cop out. He absorbs many hurts, each of which diminishes his sense of self-esteem. That only contributes to an attitude of "Why should I care about you, because you don't care about me?" At that point, either the fire goes out or it is stoked with anger and becomes the fire that destroys, not the fire that cleanses.

Cures for burnout. What is the cure? The usual advice follows these lines: exercise regularly, get proper rest, take a vacation, and reorganize your priorities. Those suggestions would undoubtedly contribute to recovery, but often the root goes deeper.

Who of us hasn't taken time to relax, only to discover we can't because of a nagging sense of guilt or failure? What about the anxiety we feel as we anticipate the next board meeting when our new proposal will be discussed? And how can you enjoy your vacation if you suspect a member of the board might undermine your leadership when you're away?

The first part of the answer to burnout is to be controlled from within rather than from without. We must be satisfied with doing the will of God rather than being overly dependent on the opinions of men. That may require getting away from it all for a week's retreat or even taking a leave of absence to get it all together. But it is in that quiet, inner world that we meet God and that the answer will eventually be found.

In *Ordering Your Private World*, Gordon MacDonald describes the difference between a person who is driven (such as King Saul) and a person who is called (such as John the Baptist). A driven person is gratified only by accomplishments and its symbols. He often possesses a volcanic anger that erupts anytime he senses opposition or disloyalty. When he cannot achieve his goals in public ministry, he becomes disillusioned because his private life is left empty and wanting.

But when news came to John the Baptist that his popularity was on the decline, he replied, "A man can receive nothing, unless it has been given him from heaven" (John 3:27).

John realized that the crowds did not belong to him; he ministered as the Lord saw fit. He didn't need the exhilaration that comes through public affirmation, nor did he see himself out of focus. He might have been tempted to think of himself as a great preacher, but he directed the crowds to Christ: "He must increase, but I must decrease" (John 3:30).

John's contentment was not built on his career; he could find stability in his private, inner world. Pastors who neglect their inner world soon find themselves unable to cope with the weight of the external demands placed upon them.

Burnout may be a reminder to develop our inner world. Spending time in quietness before the Lord and asking His guidance in those areas of neglect and failure could just be the experience we need. Perhaps those of us who say yes to too many invitations will discover we weren't called to save the world. We don't have to live up to the expectations of our congregations, but can be content serving in faithfulness within the limitations of our gifts and aptitudes.

The second part of the answer is to confide in close friends. Every pastor should have several people, perhaps outside his congregation, with whom he can be honest about his struggles. We all need the acceptance and confidentiality of friends who will listen carefully and pray fervently.

During days when we're unsteady emotionally, everything is distorted. We desperately need the perspective of those who have maintained their emotional equilibrium. Blessed is the pastor who can be open with at least a few friends during his emotional blackouts.

James B. Scott experienced burnout and resigned from his church. He wrote, "The most difficult part of the death of a dream was the feeling of loss and fear of not knowing if anything would ever come along to replace the loss." But eventually he realized that the ministry was in God's hands, not his. He continued, "Brokenness and healing has, by the power of God, produced unexpected results in my life. Strange how the pain of brokenness can miraculously bring about fullness and a tenacity of power and resources unknown previously" (*Theology News and Notes*, March 1984, p. 15).

Many of us need once again to experience the inner power of God. There in His presence we must find meaning and tranquillity within, rather than being sustained by approval from without. God wants us to find our joy coming from Him, rather than the unpredictable, often conflicting, attitudes of men.

Sometimes it may not be possible to pinpoint the cause of burnout. Even so, we must interpret it as a reminder from God that our inner life needs special attention. "In quietness and in confidence shall be your strength" (Isaiah 30:15, KJV*). C. S. Lewis says the Lord shouts to us in our pains, but, I might add, He also speaks to us in our emotional doldrums.

Jesus demonstrated an inner satisfaction that enabled Him to cope with the stresses of His ministry. When a huge crowd of people gathered to hear Him, He disappointed them by going to another town and leaving them waiting (Mark 1:37-38). When He

*King James Version.

learned that Lazarus was sick, He stayed away two extra days, knowing that the will of God was being accomplished despite the disappointment of His friends Martha and Mary (John 11:6).

Christ never seemed to be in a hurry, because He cared only about pleasing the Father. We must learn from Him the importance of playing the game for the coach, not the fickle applause of the fans.

Burnout may mean that fresh coals must be offered on the altar of the heart. The God of Elijah is able to ignite even wet wood if it is laid out before Him in submission and anticipation.

Burnout need never be permanent if we are willing to wait for God to kindle the flame.

11

The Church and the World:
Who Is Influencing Whom?

Recent Gallup polls have uncovered conflicting trends in our society: religion is on the upswing but so is crime and immorality. George Gallup calls it "a giant paradox that religion is showing clear signs of revival even as the country is ridden with rising crime and other problems regarded as antithetical to religious piety."

Addressing a national seminar of Southern Baptist leaders, Gallup said, "We find there is very little difference in ethical behavior between churchgoers and those who are not active religiously. . . . The levels of lying, cheating, and stealing are remarkably similar in both groups."

Eight out of ten Americans consider themselves Christians, Gallup said, yet only about half of them could identify the person who gave the Sermon on the Mount, and fewer still could recall five of the Ten Commandments. Only two in ten said they would be willing to suffer for their faith.

What an indictment of American Christianity to have religion up while morality is down. Let's not excuse ourselves just because we suspect that the majority of those interviewed were not born-again believers. Within evangelicalism there is a distressing drift toward accepting a Christianity that does not demand a life-changing walk with God.

Religion a la carte. Like the nominally religious, we choose what we will believe and how we will act without much concern for what the Bible teaches. Carl F. Henry wrote, "Millions of Protestants, many evangelicals among them, choose and change their churches as they do their airlines—for convenience of travel, comfort, and economy." For us, as well as for the world, it's religion a la carte.

What can account for this? Since evangelicalism became popular a few years ago, many people have felt free to identify with it at no personal cost. The stigma of Christianity is gone, but so is its power.

Within the evangelical camp, there is a growing trend toward accommodation—selecting what we like from the Bible and leaving the rest. We've been so caught up in the spirit of our age that we change colors like a chameleon to blend in with the latest worldly hue.

When gay rights activists argue that homosexuality is but an "alternate sexual preference," we find evangelicals writing books agreeing that the Bible doesn't condemn homosexuality. They say the Old Testament passages are a part of the law that doesn't apply today and that Paul was only condemning those who turned to homosexuality, not those who grew up that way.

When the feminists press their demands for equality, some preachers "restudy" the New Testament and discover that Paul didn't really mean what he wrote. They conclude that the husband is not the head of the wife and that women do have the right to be ordained. Even more frightening is one evangelical's conclusion that Paul's view of women was just plain wrong.

When a socialistic mood sweeps the country, we have Christians who advocate the application of a Marxist theory for the redistribution of wealth. And when the peace movement gains momentum, some evangelicals jump on that bandwagon, too.

I agree that we must examine our understanding of the Bible in relation to modern issues. But if we accommodate Scripture to whatever wind is blowing, we will become so absorbed by our culture that we will have nothing to say to it. In our zeal to be relevant, we will have lost our prophetic voice.

I'm reminded of the boy who bought a canary and put it in the same cage as a sparrow, hoping the sparrow would learn to sing. After three days he gave up in disgust. The sparrow didn't sound like the canary; instead, the canary sounded just like the sparrow.

In *The Great Evangelical Disaster* (Westchester, Ill.: Crossway, 1984), Francis Schaeffer says, "Here is the great evangelical disaster—the failure of the evangelical world to stand for truth as truth. . . . The evangelical church has accommodated to the world spirit of the age" (p. 37).

However much we fault German theologian Rudolf Bultmann for rejecting the parts of the Bible that did not suit his fancy, we do the same when it comes to practicing biblical truth. Our actions show us to believe that scriptural authority rests with us and not with the text.

What is the result of this accommodation that picks and chooses from a religious smorgasbord? Society is being overrun by the cults, inundated with pornography, and destroyed by abortion on demand.

There are almost as many divorces within the church as outside of it. Sexual perversions of every kind are found within the church community, too. As Gallup suggests, the ethical behavior of those who attend church and those who do not is remarkably similar.

The new philosophy that "God wants you to be rich, happy, and healthy" has appealed to a generation that is quick to accept the benefits of Christianity without painful obedience. Like a child standing by a slot machine hoping he can win the jackpot with a single coin, many churchgoers expect maximum return from minimum commitment. When they are not healed or don't get a promotion, they take their quarter and go elsewhere.

Our response. How should we respond to such an attitude? In our desire to combat easy believism, let's not add stipulations to the gospel of grace. Salvation is a gift to be received freely by simple faith. But we must explain that the Christian life has both privileges and responsibilities.

Specifically, we must point out the sin of the "me first" cult of individualism that has infected the church. We've read about the woman from a small Oklahoma congregation who took three elders to court for exercising church discipline against her. She objected to the idea of confessing her sin to the church.

After winning the suit and an amount more than the congregation's budget for six years, she declared, "I'm not saying I wasn't guilty. I was. But it was none of their business."

Submission to church leadership (Hebrews 13:17) and the clear teaching that we should not take fellow believers to court (1 Corinthians 6:1-8) were set aside in favor of personal interests. Her attorney remarked, "He was a single man. She was a single lady. And this is America." In other words, although obedience to church leaders may be laudable biblically, it is contrary to the American way of life.

How different that is from the spirit of Jesus, who pleased not Himself, but made Himself of no reputation and was obedient unto death (Romans 15:3; Philippians 2:7-8). He did it for us, but more important, He did it for God.

We must also learn that selective obedience nullifies the authority of God. We've all been tempted to neglect church discipline for fear of criticism, a charge of inconsistency, or possibly a church split. But does our well-intended negligence further the work of Christ?

Under the guise of being relevant, loving, and broad-minded, we weaken the impact of the gospel. Little wonder a member of a large evangelical church could tell me, "I can't remember the last time we've had someone saved."

As pastors, let's remember that we're not the ones who determine what we should preach, who can be remarried in our church, or what the structure of the home should be. It's not up to us to decide whether or not we should be selective in the television programs we watch, how much we should give, or whether we should witness to our neighbors. We are bondslaves of Jesus Christ, obligated to search Scripture to find an answer to the question, "Lord, what wilt Thou have me to do?"

George Gallup is optimistic. He believes that if properly nurtured, the new awareness of religion in America could bring more genuine converts into the church.

But I fear that it won't happen as long as the distinction between the church and the world remains blurred. We've come a long way from the early church, where fear fell upon the multitudes and "none of the rest dared to associate with them" (Acts 5:13).

The millions who take their religion a la carte will someday discover they've had the wrong menu. Only those who pay the price of obedience can enjoy the nourishment of the bread from heaven.

It's not the people who claim to be Christians who will affect our country; it's those who accept the cost and live the Christian life.

12

Counseling:
Must We Be Experts in Psychology?

Is a pastor without psychological training qualified to counsel his flock, or must he limit himself to spiritual counseling and refer the more difficult cases to professionals?

Many Bible school graduates think they have to get a doctorate in psychology at a state university so they can become a counselor. They think they have to combine psychological training with their Bible school knowledge for maximum effectiveness. But psychologists and theologians dispute the extent to which psychological studies can successfully integrate with the Bible.

Personally, I am wary about attempts at integration. I find no biblical support to distinguish a spiritual problem from a psychological one.

At root, man's psychological problems, unless due to physical or chemical causes, are spiritual—and where could we find a better analysis of man's need along with a supernatural remedy than in the Scriptures?

Peter writes that our Lord's divine power has granted us "everything pertaining to life and godliness, through the true knowledge of Him who called us by His own glory and excellence" (2 Peter 1:3).

Paul writes, "For in Him all the fulness of Deity dwells in bodily form, and in Him you have been made complete, and He is the head over all rule and authority" (Colossians 2:9-10). That leaves little room for using the techniques of secular psychology to help Christians achieve emotional and spiritual wholeness.

I admit, however, that God has often used Christian counselors who have built on the theories of secular psychology. God's Word is always effective regardless of the context in which it is believed and obeyed. And in some instances psychological studies have hit upon biblical truths. So psychology may have some value in helping us understand man's predicament from a different perspective.

Lawrence Crabb, in his book *Effective Biblical Counseling,* advocates that we "spoil the Egyptians"—we should use the insights, principles, and techniques of psychology that are consistent with Scripture to help us become more effective. I appreciate his desire to test the presuppositions of secular theories so that we would accept only what is biblical.

But even then, I suspect that if we'd take the time to analyze the text, we would find that such psychological insights are already in the Scriptures.

A biblical approach. It's unfortunate that the expression "biblical counseling" has a negative connotation. Some think it means that the antidote to every problem is just information, and the relationship between the counselor and the counselee is therefore mechanistic and impersonal.

A thoroughly biblical approach rejects such a simplistic notion.

Paul stressed the personal dimension in exhortation and encouragement. He fathered those who needed discipline and mothered those who needed tender care (1 Thessalonians 2:7).

A reflective knowledge of the Scriptures along with a compassionate heart can, under the guidance of the Spirit, be used to uncover the root cause of problems that elude a purely psychological approach.

A familiar story from the Old Testament illustrates the point. In Joshua 7, Israel lost thirty-six men when trying to conquer Ai. What would a secular analyst say about that ignominious defeat?

That the army used the wrong strategy? That the weapons were outdated? That too few men were sent to the battle zone?

Incredibly, military matters had nothing to do with Israel's defeat. God said the reason was that a man had stolen some items and hidden them in his tent (Joshua 7:10-12). One man's sin indicted others.

God established a cause-effect relationship that defies scientific analysis. Secular man often fails to uncover the true nature of a problem because the cause may lie entirely outside his investigation. Spiritual causes are discovered only by those with scriptural insight into the ways of God and His dealings with men.

If I had been telling the story of Achan, I would have said, "Achan sinned." But God's commentary says, "The sons of Israel acted unfaithfully" (7:1). Israel was a spiritual commonwealth bound together by a covenant.

A similar relationship exists between members of a family. "I, the Lord your God, am a jealous God, visiting the iniquity of the fathers on the children, on the third and fourth generations of those who hate me" (Exodus 20:5).

When Ham acted indecently, his son Canaan was cursed (Genesis 9:25). Demons may harass a family line, and hence a child may be afflicted (Mark 9:20-21). In such cases the influence of the parents and grandparents must be broken. Perhaps that is why the people of Israel confessed the sins of their fathers (Nehemiah 9:2).

Conversely, blessings may often be attributed to godly influences. The Lord shows "lovingkindness to thousands, to those who love [Him] and keep [His] commandments" (Exodus 20:6).

Solomon was spared judgment because of his father David's sake (1 Kings 11:12). Laban was blessed because of Jacob (Genesis 30:27). And an unbelieving marriage partner is set apart for spiritual privileges because of a believing spouse (1 Corinthians 7:14).

Concerning the Body of Christ, Paul wrote, "If one member suffers, all the members suffer with it; if one member is honored, all the members rejoice with it" (1 Corinthians 12:26).

The consequences of sin. When a fellow believer falls into sin, part of the responsibility may be ours. Paul said the whole Body suffers. If one member is spiritually cold, he lowers the temperature of everyone around him.

Spiritual power is unleashed when the church diffuses its strength throughout the whole Body. Believers have overcome depression, forgiven abusive parents, and developed wholesome self-images when the Body provides love and acceptance. Fractured personalities can be put back together within the context of people who see another's failure as their own.

No one counsels with a sense of detachment when he realizes that failure is a shared experience. When a family breaks up, we all hurt. My first response to a believer's defeat should be to search my own heart.

Such an understanding of Scripture does not absolve individuals of responsibility. We are not programmed by the performances of others. God has tempered parental influence with personal responsibility (Ezekiel 18:20).

The human family owes a huge debt to God; we bear its burden both corporately and individually. The warriors who went to capture Ai would have had a greater concern for Achan's spiritual life if they had remembered that his actions were bound up with theirs.

Personal sin is also interrelated. The works of the flesh come in clusters. We cannot tolerate sin in one part of our life and be experiencing victory in another. If we close one room of our life to God, darkness settles over the whole house.

One man who struggled with pornography could not overcome his secret sin until he made restoration for items he had stolen many years ago. Another overcame cigarette smoking after he asked his parents to forgive him for the rebellion of his youth, when he had begun the habit against their wishes.

In marriage counseling I've sometimes asked a couple if they had premarital sex.

"What difference does that make?" they retort. But if they have, they've planted seeds that have borne bitter fruit. They've forgotten that you never reap in the same season that you sow.

Sin sprouts roots in any number of unpredictable directions. If covetousness can lead to the defeat of an army, might not cheating on one's income tax lead to excessive anger or even immorality? James says that a double-minded man is unstable in all his ways.

This knowledge of sin's effects ought to influence our counseling. We must see failure in its larger context and take time for spiritual inventory.

How might we have failed our brothers and sisters in Christ? What hidden sins within a family or church might have provided the climate for marital strife, moral sin, or emotional turbulence? I must ask God to search my heart and then seek His wisdom to identify the cause of personal and corporate defeat.

I believe that if Joshua had come to God before he sent men to Ai, the Lord would have revealed Achan's secret sin, and Israel would have been spared defeat. But Joshua acted hastily. Even on a later occasion, he got into trouble by not seeking the counsel of the Lord (Joshua 9).

When unconfessed sin is found, it must be judged. Achan and his family were stoned and then burned (Joshua 7:25). A heap of stones was left in the valley of Achor as a memorial of that shameful event, and "the Lord turned from the fierceness of His anger" (7:26).

Once sin was put away, Joshua and his men defeated Ai, apparently without the loss of a single soldier. When sin is judged, blessing flows.

Let no one say that my theory of counseling is simply to hunt for hidden sin. In some instances the cause may be sin in general; no specific sin needs to be confessed.

An abused child, for example, needs unconditional love and acceptance. His emotional problems will not likely be helped by trying to uncover hidden sins, though forgiveness toward his parents will become necessary at some point.

But often God does judge us as individuals and as churches because we have been unwilling to make a thorough housecleaning of our lives. The Holy Spirit is willing to search our hearts when we become honest (Psalm 139:23-24).

Achor means "trouble," an apparent reference to the severe judgment that Achan and his family received there. But hundreds of years later, the prophet Hosea says that the valley of Achor will be a door of hope (Hosea 2:15). Hidden sin becomes a place of judgment; when confessed and forsaken, that place becomes a door of hope.

Every pastor must be comfortable with his own philosophy of counseling, but I suspect that we'd all be more successful if we sought God's wisdom in uncovering the causes of spiritual failure. God wants to build a monument of victory in the valley of defeat, and He's given us the tools to help Him.

13
Worship: Can It Happen
in a Structured Service?

As a new bride, a woman in a remote village dreamed about the security and happiness her marriage would bring. Perhaps her expectations were unrealistic. Maybe she was too preoccupied with her own ambitions to recognize the first signs of tension in her marriage.

But the tensions mushroomed. Eventually she and her husband agreed they could not live together any longer. The decision was agonizing but from all appearances necessary. They were divorced.

Time heals all wounds, or at least lessens the pain. After the woman had pulled herself together emotionally, she met a man who seemed to have all the qualities her first husband lacked. *This* marriage would be a success.

When her second marriage showed signs of strain, the woman dared not let herself think it would end like the first. Yet, the foundations of that relationship began to crumble. Before long, the woman experienced a second divorce.

Some women would have buried their frustrations in a career. They would have relocated in another city, gone back to school, or learned a skill. But this woman could not. Her family believed not only that a woman's place was at home but also that she was to be obedient to the whims of her husband. Furthermore, in her locality, no jobs were available to women. All she knew—all she could know—were household chores, the drudgery of routine.

The decision to marry the third time was made more easily. By that time, the woman was bitter at God and disgruntled with men. If her marriage didn't work, another divorce would rescue her from the bonds of meaningless vows. Predictably, she experienced a third divorce. Then a fourth and a fifth.

When she met another man, she decided not to bother with the formality of a wedding. They just lived together under common law.

And then she met Jesus Christ, who offered her living water. He also invited her to worship the Most High God.

"Our fathers worshiped in this mountain," she offered.

"Woman, believe Me," Christ replied, "an hour is coming when neither in this mountain, nor in Jerusalem, shall you worship the Father. . . . But an hour is coming, and now is, when the true worshipers shall worship the Father in spirit and truth; for such people the Father seeks to be His worshipers" (John 4: 21, 23).

The essence of worship. "To worship," said William Temple, Archbishop of Canterbury from 1942 to 1944, "is to quicken the conscience by the holiness of God, to feed the mind with the truth of God, to purge the imagination by the beauty of God, to pen the heart to the love of God, and to devote the will to the purpose of God" (cited in John MacArthur, *The Ultimate Priority* [Chicago: Moody, 1983], p. 147).

The woman at the well considered worship a matter of outward conformity. But Christ taught that it was a matter of spirit and truth. The Jews worshiped in Jerusalem, the Samaritans on Mount Gerizim. Now worship would not be confined to geography. It was no longer a matter of being in the Temple or on the right hilltop.

How often we assume that we must be in church to worship. We are told that the church building is "God's house." That is an inaccurate designation borrowed from the Old Testament Temple. God was displeased with the Temple worship in Jerusalem. He is equally unimpressed with our cathedral worship today.

Worship isn't listening to a sermon, appreciating choir music, or joining to sing hymns. In fact, it isn't even necessarily prayer, for prayer sometimes comes from an unbroken, unyielded heart. Worship is not an external activity precipitated by the right environment.

To worship in spirit is to draw near to God with an undivided heart. We must come in full agreement without hiding anything or disregarding His will. Augustine spoke of those who have tried unsuccessfully to find God. "They were probably inflated by their pride of learning and so were misled into seeking Him by throwing out their chests rather than beating upon their breasts."

Leading others to worship. How can we as pastors help our people worship? First we must stress that worship demands preparation. A person cannot worship in church if he has not met the Lord before arriving at the door.

The sixty minutes before Sunday school and church is, for many Christians, the most unholy hour of the week. Eating, dressing, and scurrying around the house to finish those last-minute tasks and then driving to church out-of-sorts with one another is not conducive to a prepared heart. What we do before the service will determine what happens within it.

The form of worship is not as important as the spiritual condition of the human heart. John MacArthur, Jr., wrote in *The Ultimate Priority,* "If our corporate worship isn't the expression of our individual worshiping lives, it is unacceptable. If you think you can live any way you want and then go to church on Sunday morning and turn on worship with the saints, you're wrong" (p. 104).

David said, "Unite my heart to fear Thy name" (Psalm 86:11). Our congregations must also come to God single-mindedly, in full agreement.

Second, we must worship in truth. Worship is not just an emotional exercise but a response of the heart built on truth about God. "The Lord is near to all who call upon Him, to all who call upon Him in truth" (Psalm 145:18). Worship not based on God's Word is but an emotional encounter with oneself.

Remember what happened when Nehemiah asked Ezra to read the scrolls of Scripture? "Then Ezra blessed the Lord the great God. And all the people answered, 'Amen, amen!' while lifting up their hands; then they bowed low and worshiped the Lord with their faces to the ground" (Nehemiah 8:6). The truth of God in their minds led the Israelites to bow their knees in worship.

In his book *Between Two Worlds* (Grand Rapids: Eerdmans, 1982), John Stott says, "Word and worship belong indissolubly to each other. All worship is an intelligent and loving response to the revelation of God, because it is the adoration of His name. Therefore, acceptable worship is impossible without preaching. For preaching is making known the name of the Lord, and worship is praising the name of the Lord made known" (p. 82-83).

There can be no worship without obedience to truth. That's why worship often involves sacrifice. It's not just praising God but praising Him through our instant response to His requests.

When Abraham was asked to sacrifice Isaac, he said to his young men, "Stay here with the donkey, and I and the lad will go yonder; and we will worship and return to you" (Genesis 22:5). Abraham expected to slay his son, yet he called that worship.

Our parishioners cannot worship in church unless they have made some hard choices for God during the week. To speak of worship without surrender is like expecting an airplane to fly with one wing.

The people in Isaiah's day were not condemned because they sang the wrong songs. God did not judge them because they prayed unorthodox prayers. The nation even brought sacrifices. But they lacked surrendered hearts. Christ, quoting Isaiah, said, "You hypocrites, rightly did Isaiah prophesy of you, saying, 'This people honors me with their lips, but their heart is far away from Me. But in vain do they worship Me, teaching as their doctrines the precepts of men'" (Matthew 15:7-9).

Talk is cheap. It's obedience to truth that really matters. That's why worship is always costly. It means we come before God with a signed blank check.

Finally, Christ said that worship is a matter of priority. "The Father seeks such people to worship Him." At first glance, that seems odd. Would not all men, especially Christians, want to worship the Father? Would it not be natural for us, the creatures, to want to meet our Creator? Yet, it's Almighty God who does the seeking. My guess is that there are relatively few who respond.

How can we entice our people to take God up on His offer? For one thing, we must be worshipers ourselves. If we don't schedule time to worship God with meaning, we can't expect our congregations to do it either. Ann Ortlund wrote, "A congregation doesn't become broken because the minister tells them to. They get broken when he gets broken."

Second, we must concentrate on sharing with our people the glories of who God is. We should let them know that the Christian life is more than seeking freedom from sin.

Christians must also long to draw closer to God. If we are quenching our thirst at forbidden fountains, we have no reason to expect God to be satisfying. If we are not nourished by the bread from heaven, we will satiate ourselves with crumbs from the world. Once we have become addicted to the world's nourishment, our appetite for God is spoiled.

How can this apply to next Sunday morning? Pastors are not actors performing on stage for a crowd of staid bystanders. Rather, the whole congregation must participate while God, our audience, watches to see how well we do. He's monitoring us to find those whose hearts are perfect toward Him.

Let's begin by asking: How can we lift our congregations into God's presence and leave them there to cry, praise, and enjoy? Do we emphasize that they are actually on stage before God? Is there planned spontaneity, where the Lord is free to do something not listed in the bulletin?

God gave the privilege of worship to an immoral woman. Regardless of her past failures, worship was an exciting possibility. He now extends the same invitation to us, R.S.V.P.

OF course you can be saved without walking an aisle, but don't say you heard it from me.

14

Public Invitations:
Are We Being Misunderstood?

"Those who want to accept Christ as Savior, please leave your seats and come and stand at the front of the platform." Most of us have heard invitations like that ever since we were children.

In some churches, abandoning the invitation would be considered the first step toward liberalism. Even those who feel that "coming forward" has no biblical support still practice regular public invitations and would never dream of changing them.

In the minds of many, having people come forward proves that the pastor is evangelistic and that God is at work. Regardless of what happens in the counseling room, the fact that there has been an outward sign gives the congregation the feeling that the church is on the move.

But this past summer, as I sat on a park bench and heard a young preacher urge people to come forward to receive Christ, I realized once again our urgent need to rethink our method of giving invitations. No matter how accustomed to it we may be, we must subject our practice to vigorous biblical scrutiny.

Charles Finney was among the first evangelists to call people forward during a service. He defended the practice by saying it served the same purpose as baptism in the days of the apostles.

But he was putting the cart before the horse; baptism must be a sign that one has been converted, not a prerequisite for conversion. Ever since Finney's time, public invitations have generated similar misunderstandings.

In some churches, walking forward and "coming to Christ" are linked to the point that people are led to believe one can't happen without the other. To come forward is to "come to Jesus."

What happens when we associate these two separate acts? First, it perpetuates the notion that walking before a crowd has some special merit in the conversion process. Those who are afraid to go forward may actually think they cannot be saved.

When I was ten years old, I was too embarrassed to walk in front of several hundred people. So I suffered through those invitations where we sang all the stanzas of a hymn a half dozen times. Meanwhile, I was thinking, *If I have to go forward in front of all these people, I'll just have to go to hell.*

Misconceptions about invitations. Although evangelists privately admit that a person can be saved without going forward, many do not want the word to get around. Saying, "Why don't you leave your seat and come to receive Christ?" is carefully calculated to urge people to respond physically to their appeal.

One evangelist obscures the issues even more by saying he wants to make it hard for people to respond to Christ. He derides this generation's "easy believism"; he wants to make faith tough. For him, the place to begin is by walking forward in front of the whole congregation. Taking Christ's invitation to discipleship as an invitation to salvation, he insists that people walk forward publicly to be saved.

Another preacher says he wants to give people an opportunity to "demonstrate" for Jesus Christ: "People are demonstrating for everything today; why don't you get out of your seat and demonstrate for Christ?"

He thought he was making it difficult to become a Christian, but actually he was making it easy. There is nothing repulsive to the flesh about demonstrating for a worthy cause. Little wonder that when a counselor asked a young man why he had come forward his unhesitating reply was, "Because the world's in a mess, and I want to help."

Yes, it is difficult to become a Christian. But the difficulty is in acknowledging our sin and helplessness—precisely what proud hearts are unwilling to do. It's hard to admit that we must cast ourselves on the mercy of God in Jesus Christ. The difficulty is with the blindness of the human heart and an unwillingness to see our own condition before God.

Making it appear as if walking forward is the hard part obscures the issues of the gospel. It mixes faith and works and gives the impression that being willing to come forward is somehow related to being willing to come to Christ.

I cringed when I heard a person who attends a church that gives such invitations say, "I want to be saved, but I'll have to wait until next Sunday."

This popular misconception about invitations not only adds the requirement of works to the gospel but also puts assurance on a wrong foundation. Many today think they are saved because they have gone forward to "receive Christ."

Somehow the natural man feels that if he hasn't performed a saving act, he has at least contributed to it. Because of his heart's blindness and deception, he feels he must do the best he can to repair his relationship with God. And afterward he prides himself in having had the courage to do so.

I've often heard a Christian who should know better say, "Wasn't it great to see three people saved this morning?" Because three people went forward during the invitation, they assume regeneration has taken place. But someone can go forward, pray an appropriate prayer, and still leave unconverted.

Yet this style of invitation is sometimes defended because it makes good psychology: people should make some kind of response to "nail down" their decision.

That sounds reasonable, but it breeds confusion. Those who haven't gone forward may think they cannot be saved, and those who have gone forward think they are saved because of their courageous act of walking in front of several hundred people.

Dr. Lewis Sperry Chafer, founder of Dallas Theological Seminary, frequently gave invitations in the early years of his ministry.

But he eventually concluded that they obscured the issues of the gospel. He said, "Careful students of evangelism have noticed that where the necessity of public action as a part of conversion has been most emphasized there has been a corresponding increase in the God-dishonoring record of so-called 'backsliding'; and this is natural" (*True Evangelism* [Grand Rapids: Zondervan], p. 15). The reason is obvious. Unconverted people think they are saved simply because they came forward.

I realize, however, that many have received Christ as Savior when they responded to an altar call. Some even say that deciding to walk forward was a test of their sincerity in surrendering to the Holy Spirit's conviction. But we should never give the impression that the two actions are inseparably linked.

A balanced approach. God's part in salvation is to convict the sinner, draw him, and grant him the gift of repentance. All man can do is to respond to what God is doing and cast himself upon God's mercy that he might be saved. To associate that with the act of coming forward in a meeting is to dilute the purity of the gospel and to focus on the wrong issue.

It's not whether a man is willing to walk in front of other people that is important to God. It's whether he is willing to acknowledge his sin and receive the mercy that God extends to him through the cross.

As Chafer said, "The one necessary step—the acceptance of Christ as Savior—can be performed only in the secret of the heart itself, by a personal choice and action of the will. This is a dealing with Christ alone, and as the time of this decision is the most critical moment in a human life, reason demands that it should be guarded from every distracting and confusing condition" (*True Evangelism*, p. 14-15).

Giving an invitation to the unconverted has also led to the embarrassment of large numbers of apparent converts coming forward and then failing to show spiritual fruit in their lives. We could be spared this questioning of the power of the gospel if we waited for the fruit of repentance, rather than counting converts based on the outward sign of walking forward.

We must continue, however, to call men and women to come to Christ. Whenever possible—publicly or privately—we should urge men and women to repentance and faith. But that is the key. They should come to Christ, rather than to the front of a church or to a counselor or an evangelist.

There is a place for invitations. It is appropriate to give Christians an opportunity to confess Christ or invite people to receive spiritual counsel.

Paul wrote, "If you confess with your mouth Jesus as Lord, and believe in your heart that God raised Him from the dead, you shall be saved; for with the heart man believes, resulting in righteousness, and with the mouth he confesses, resulting in salvation" (Romans 10:9-10).

But that passage cannot be interpreted to mean that regeneration comes about by a public confession. Such an understanding would disagree with scores of other passages.

Verse 9 must be interpreted in the light of verse 10. How is a right standing gained before God? "With the heart man believeth unto righteousness" (v. 10, KJV). It is in the heart that the will, exercised by the Holy Spirit, responds to the saving work of Christ.

The confession "unto salvation" is a result of having received the gift of righteousness. Thus the believer testifies with his mouth to what God has wrought in his heart.

If we give people an opportunity to receive Christ while they are still seated in the congregation, we can invite them to share their decision with the pastor after the service. That also provides an opportunity to give further counsel.

We could also make an effort to separate the physical response from the spiritual act of conversion. At Moody Church, I invite people to the front so they can discuss a spiritual need with a member of the pastoral staff or a counselor. It provides an opportunity to pray, ask questions, and receive spiritual counsel —whether one is saved or unsaved.

Let's not associate the act of walking forward with "coming to Christ," and let's not be afraid to tell people that they can be saved where they are seated—or wherever they might find themselves next week. They don't have to wait until next Sunday.

We must urge people to come—not to the preacher, the platform, or a counselor—but to the invisible Christ.

15
God's Judgment:
How Can We Recognize It Today?

At a recent meeting of religious leaders, one respected observer of the American political scene remarked, "We've lost the abortion battle in Washington. Now there's no turning back . . . we are sliding toward the judgment of God."

I'm not qualified to say that the fight against abortion is dead politically, nor can I put a timetable on God's judgment. But we cannot escape the consequences of killing four thousand unborn babies every day.

It's popular to blame the Supreme Court, the humanists, and the radical feminists. To be sure, they have contributed to the abortion holocaust. But if God is using them to judge us, might not the responsibility more properly be laid at the feet of those who know the living God but who have failed to influence society?

If we were few in number, we could more easily evade censure. But there are tens of thousands of evangelical pastors in America who lead several million born-again believers. And yet we're losing one battle after another. Perhaps the church doesn't suffer for the sins of the world as much as the world suffers for the sins of the church.

Because of our cowardly silence in the midst of abortion, pornography, and the erosion of our religious liberties, and because of our acceptance of compromise within the church, the salt has lost its savor and the light flickers.

Each of us is indicted. We're afraid to speak out or to identify with pro-life groups, because we don't want to be characterized as bigoted or outdated. But by our silence we have contributed to the death of millions of unborn babies and many more who are allowed to starve to death because of some physical handicap.

Where have we failed? First, we have neglected the unconverted. We give our lives to an evangelical subculture that our neighbors don't even know exists, except for the information they receive through the media.

If each Christian family led one person to Christ per year (we expect at least ten times that from our missionaries) and discipled that individual, our impact among the unconverted would be phenomenal. Yet we are told that 95 percent of all Christians have never given a clear witness to an unsaved neighbor. However much we may talk about the power of the gospel, we are apparently frightened to share it.

Second, we have retreated behind what Francis Schaeffer calls "false pietism" in regard to social issues. We have eschewed anything that necessitates sacrificial involvement. We've neglected to do good to all men, even to those who are of the household of faith. As long as we live well, can choose our friends, and are assured a comfortable retirement, we don't care too much about newspaper headlines. What matters is that our personal peace and affluence not be disrupted.

Of course we may preach an occasional sermon against abortion, but are we willing to help teenage girls who are pregnant? We may condemn injustice, but are we willing to use our own finances and influences to help those who have been treated unfairly? Talk is cheap. It's easy to say the right words and then hope that someone else will fight our battles.

Also, we have accepted the world's values in entertainment, leisure, and success. We have lost our ability to critique society. Since the church is so often indistinguishable from the world, the unconverted have no model of righteousness.

Every Christian couple that divorces causes others to question the power of God. When a church splits over a trivial matter, it says to the community that God cannot bring restoration and forgiveness to His people. When fathers neglect to lead their families in prayer and Bible instruction, they subtly give the impression that God's counsel is optional! And when we are willing to rationalize sensuality, selfishness, and greed, we are in effect admitting that Christ is unable to free us from sin. As a result, we have nothing to say to this generation.

What form will God's judgment take? Usually we imagine judgment coming in the form of war with Russia or famine, but those are not the only possibilities. After God warned the Israelites of famines, wars, and boils, He predicted that the final judgment would be captivity. "Your sons and your daughters shall be given to another people, while your eyes shall look on and yearn for them continually; but there shall be nothing you can do" (Deuteronomy 28:32). The severest judgment was the scattering of Israel's families.

Though in a different way, the same thing is happening to us today. One-half of all children born this year will at some time live with only a single parent. As our homes continue to break up, depression, hatred, and child abuse result. Such consequences of disobedience will escalate.

Or perhaps God's judgment will include intensifying emotional disorders. He told the Israelites that their disobedience would bring "despair of soul" (Deuteronomy 28:65). Unresolved guilt surfaces under different labels—anger, insensitivity, depression. With millions of women having abortions and an equal and even greater number of men guilty of sexual immorality, future generations will find mental illness on the increase. We can expect that our nation will rot from within.

What can we do? The only hope for America can be found in the church. The Body of Christ still wields awesome power. If we

are brought to our knees, God may begin to give us spiritual victories that could stem abortion, infanticide, and drug abuse.

When Mordecai told Esther that she should go before the
king to intercede for the Jews, she hesitated, fearing for her own
life. But Mordecai replied, "Do not imagine that you in the king's
palace can escape any more than all the Jews. . . . And who
knows whether you have not attained royalty for such a time as
this?" (Esther 4:13-14).

Esther had to be willing to lay her life on the line before deliverance would come. She couldn't feel content because of her
own supposed security. In the end, it wasn't the rooms of an opu-
lent palace but only God who could save her. So she risked her
life, saying, "If I perish, I perish." Only at such costs did God
bring deliverance.

Though Esther and the Jews were a minority, that mattered
little when God took up their cause.

Our political options in fighting abortion appear to be limit-
ed, but that is not a cause for discouragement. What the Supreme
Court thinks is meaningless when God fights in behalf of His
people.

Perhaps God is trying to teach us that we cannot depend on
human agencies to turn this nation back to Him. We must wait
before Him until He gives us the grace to weep for our nation and
its leaders. We must repent of our comfortable relationship with
the world. We must grieve not so much for ungodly men who
make unjust laws, but for the people of God who are spiritually
paralyzed and unable to witness to Christ's power in every sphere
of life.

God is willing to meet us, but, even at this late hour, I'm not
sure that we are ready to pay the price.

If we are desperate as we profess to be, I propose that we as
pastors:

- Do whatever God may require in order to restore our
  authority.

- Spend one day a week in prayer and fasting for ourselves, our churches, and our nation.
- Pray that God might remove those in courts and government responsible for unjust laws.
- Influence as many people as we can for the cause of Christ and the gospel.

Our time is short. Our political and legal options are beginning to close. We are on the way down.

Only God can save us now.

16

Christian Humanism:
Old or New?

Listen to some evangelicals and you'll be led to believe that man does not exist for God's benefit, but God exists for the benefit of man. Man tells God when he wants to be saved, how rich he'd like to become, and even his own version of theology.

The clay is giving the Potter instructions.

We've been seeing trends in this direction for some time. Many evangelicals have left the Reformation doctrines of total depravity, the bondage of the human will, and man's need for sovereign grace. In their place a man-centered theology substitutes a general commitment to Christ for repentance; emotional feelings replace worship.

I agree with Joe Bayly, who wrote, "In our 'let's give God a hand' (applaud, everyone) Christian culture, we have lost a sense of wonder, of awe, of approaching an Almighty God when we pray. Even our worship is narcissistic."

A new theology. This theological climate has given birth to books like Robert Schuller's *Self-Esteem—The New Reformation* (Word, 1982). Although it was appropriate for Calvin and Luther to think theocentrically, because in their day everyone was in the church, Schuller says times have changed: "What we need is a theology of salvation that begins and ends with a recognition of every person's hunger for glory" (pp. 26-27).

Sin, traditionally thought to be against God, is now defined as against man: "any act or thought that robs myself or another human being of his or her self-esteem" (p. 14).

The differences between the sixteenth-century Reformation and this new reformation are obvious. Gone is the idea that a knowledge of God is one's highest goal; a knowledge of ourselves and of our need for self-respect is now the first item on the theological agenda.

God is not so much a judge who has been offended but a servant who is waiting for an opportunity to affirm our dignity. We come to Him on the basis of our self-worth rather than the blood of Christ.

How then shall we present this gospel? Schuller says that Christ never called anyone a sinner. "The Gospel message is not only faulty, but potentially dangerous if it has to put a person down before it attempts to lift him up," he says (p. 127). In effect, we stand before God to be exalted, not to be abased.

This reformation, then, is basically a call to a new preoccupation with ourselves rather than with God. But, unfortunately, as man is lifted up, God is dethroned.

Let's not think, however, that Schuller's book is an isolated case of Christian humanism. The fact that some so-called evangelicals accept this new reformation is proof enough that man-centered theology has permeated high places. I'm afraid that all of us have been affected.

The consequences. What are the consequences of such thinking? First, theology itself becomes relative.

We agree that it's proper to begin a message or book with an emphasis on human need as an attention-getter. Good preaching brings the turbulent predicament of man and the unchangeable grace of God together.

But Schuller's proposal goes beyond that. His theology is based in part on the opinion poll. Since people want to hear something positive, Schuller gives it to them.

Can you imagine Isaiah asking the people of Judah what they'd like to hear before he prepared his sermon? Or Christ tailoring His message to suit the Pharisees' hunger for personal glory?

It's easy to recognize the extremes, but we as pastors also ought to plead guilty to preaching what is popular rather than what is true. We sometimes skirt church discipline, the biblical standards for church leadership, and the Scriptures' denunciation of materialism for fear of rocking the ecclesiastical boat. Why alienate those who pay your salary? A bugle call is an unwelcome irritation to those at ease in Zion.

How easy it is to exchange "Thus saith the Lord" for "Thus saith psychology" or even "Thus saith the church board." Pastors are called by God to stand apart from our society, to preach the Word of God whether it's what people want to hear or not.

God's absolute justice, mercy, and love along with Christ's substitutionary atonement can never be compromised to accommodate the current psychology of the day. We can't criticize the world's relativism if we have a relativism of our own.

Second, man-centered theology leads to incomplete repentance.

What is the basis on which we approach God? Our inherent value as persons or Christ's sacrifice on the cross?

For the Christian humanist, man's sin is not so much an offense to God as it is an offense to man. Because we are valuable unconditionally, God is waiting to accept us. The assumption is that He owes us something; we do not come as undeserving sinners.

How different is the teaching of the Bible. Yes, we have dignity as persons; but, because we are corrupt, God owes us nothing. If we get what we deserve, we'll be in hell forever. So we come in humility, recognizing that whatever God gives us is a gift —an undeserved favor. And the basis of our coming is the blood of Christ, not our value as persons.

I've found that incomplete repentance often leads to resentment against God. The logic is obvious: If He exists for my benefit, what happens when my "hunger for glory" remains unsatisfied?

Humans are notorious for insisting on their "rights." If we don't see ourselves as undeserving sinners, we'll be upset when God doesn't do what we think He ought.

Job initially felt that way. He believed that if he served God faithfully, blessings ought to follow. When tragedy came, his wife suggested, "Curse God and die." She thought that God owed her happiness.

But at the end of the book Job comes to full repentance. God owed him nothing—not even an explanation for his suffering. When he saw God, he abhorred himself and said, "I repent in dust and ashes" (Job 42:6).

No one repents unless he sees himself as undeserving. If I am worthy of God's blessing, grace is diminished. It's our corruption yet His acceptance of us through Christ that magnifies His grace.

Third, our impact in society is diluted.

We've all heard about the resurgence of evangelicalism in the last decade. Yet its influence in society is declining. Religion is up, but morality is down.

Recently I heard a report that the TV viewing habits of Christians and non-Christians are practically indistinguishable. In our desire to be heard by the world, we have lost our motivation to be separate from it. Our witness for Christ has a hollow ring.

Might not our impotency be traced to an exaggerated view of man's ability to the detriment of God's sovereignty? One reason Jonathan Edwards and George Whitefield had such widespread impact is because they insisted that the human heart is in a state of total corruption apart from the gracious intervention of God.

Such preaching confronted men and women with their needs. Sinners cried to God for mercy that they might not be consumed by His wrath. Conversion was not a decision made leisurely, but people sought God to "make their calling and election sure."

Someone has said that the marks of a strong church are wet eyes, bent knees, and a broken heart. We'll never be powerful until we let God be God and jealously guard His honor.

Our responsibility. How can we stem the drift toward a man-centered approach to theology? Let's set aside the new reformation and return to the old one. Let's not shrink from preaching the unpopular doctrines of Paul—the total depravity of man and the spiritual deadness of the unconverted.

We should not blush to admit with Luther and Calvin that repentance is a gift of God, granted to those who cast themselves on His mercy. The worship of God is man's highest calling. Indeed, creation exists for His good pleasure.

This traditional emphasis leads us to self-understanding. Far from stripping us of dignity, such exaltation of God would help us to see ourselves as He sees us.

King Nebuchadnezzar saw himself as Christian humanists would recommend today: he had self-confidence, esteem, and, apparently, an integrated personality. He was a positive thinker whose great plans were realized.

"Is this not Babylon the great, which I myself have built as a royal residence by the might of my power and for the glory of my majesty?" he asked (Daniel 4:30). His hunger for glory was satisfied.

God's response was to smite him with insanity. Nebuchadnezzar lived with the beasts of the field and ate grass like the cattle. His hair grew like eagles' feathers and his nails like birds' claws.

That experience delivered him from a distorted view of himself. When he finally saw himself as he was before God, his sanity and position as king were restored.

He then "blessed the Most High and praised and honored Him who lives forever; for His dominion is an everlasting dominion, and His kingdom endures from generation to generation. And all the inhabitants of the earth are accounted as nothing, but

He does according to His will in the host of heaven and among the inhabitants of the earth; and no one can ward off His hand or say to Him, 'What hast Thou done?'" (Daniel 4:34-35).

He understood that God came first in theology.

Thereafter, God blessed him, because he knew that he was the clay and God was the Potter. In our slide toward narcissistic preoccupation with ourselves rather than God, it's a truth we need to reaffirm.

17

Priorities:
How Can I Get My Act Together?

No pastor wants to climb the ladder of success only to discover that his ladder was leaning against the wrong wall!

We all want to end with the satisfaction that we have done not just good things but those that were best. In serving Christ, Martha did what was beneficial, but Jesus pointed out that she had neglected the one thing that was needful. Despite her good intentions, she had a problem with priorities.

Success is a series of right choices. Each day we stand at a fork in the road. When we say yes to one activity we must say no to another. A night out with the family means we disappoint the hospital patient who thinks a visit from the pastor is overdue. Saying yes to a luncheon means less time for study.

"Effective leadership," Ted Engstrom says, "is the willingness to sacrifice for the sake of predetermined objectives." We've got to know what we want to achieve and then go for it with single-minded determination. As D. L. Moody said, "This one thing I do . . . not these forty things I dabble in."

But what should our priorities be? How should our time be spent when there is an endless array of good things from which we must choose?

Each pastor has to determine the specifics for himself. There is no one right answer to the question of how much time to spend each week in counseling versus visitation. Those matters will be determined by the size of your church, your gifts, and the expectations of your congregation.

But there are basic principles that should guide us regardless of our specific job descriptions. The following list of priorities helps me sort out the many options that confront all of us in ministry.

Praying is more important than preaching. I don't mean we must give more time to prayer than study—though there might be times when that would be profitable. What I mean is that we must guard our time for prayer even more closely than our time for study. When we're forced to choose, prayer should get top priority.

That was true of Christ, who spent a large part of His ministry in prayer. One day, His miracles so astonished the crowd that the whole city gathered at the door. It was a pastor's dream; people were everywhere. The next morning, Christ arose early and went to a secluded place to pray. Peter and some of the other disciples interrupted Him, saying, "Everyone is looking for you!" (Mark 1:37).

What would we have done? We'd have turned to Capernaum to meet the expectations of the crowd. But Christ said to His disciples, "Let us go somewhere else—to the nearby villages—so I can preach there also. That is why I have come."

Because He had other responsibilities, He left the multitude disappointed. He refused to let the crowd dictate His schedule. Prayer in the morning hours was more important than ministry.

Jesus taught that men ought always to pray and not faint, implying we have to do one or the other. Though he may be naturally gifted, a man of God must develop through travail in prayer.

Though we ought to spend much time preparing our minds for preaching, great men of the past have often spent the same amount of time in prayer, preparing their souls. Prayer, it is said, is not the preparation for the work, it *is* the work.

If your prayer life is mediocre or inconsistent, your first priority is to set aside time for prayer. It doesn't have to be in the morning; I have mine in the afternoon. You might want to begin with fifteen minutes or half an hour. But whatever you do, make it such a priority that only an emergency would make you miss your appointment.

Preaching is more important than administration. Many pastors spend so much time running the church that they have little time for study and reflection.

The temptation is to spend most of our time in our "comfort zones." The one who enjoys study often ignores administration; the one who thrives on administration tends to neglect study. Blessed is the church whose pastor has both gifts.

Committees are necessary. Even more important is vision and the ability to move the congregation toward the goals of the church. But when push comes to shove, it's the ministry of the Word that gives us our greatest impact.

A church can usually put up with weak administration if it has effective preaching. But there's nothing quite as pathetic as people coming to a church and returning home without spiritual food.

One way to carve more time out of a busy day is to exercise the art of delegation. Ask yourself what you are doing that someone else could do; be generous in giving away all the responsibilities you reasonably can. That will save you several hours per week. Have we forgotten that no one person has all the gifts, that the Lord has places for others in the Body?

The wise pastor will concentrate on his strengths and delegate other responsibilities. One of your strengths should be preaching. Give it top priority.

The family is more important than the congregation. This has been stressed so often that it scarcely needs to be mentioned. But many of us still have not got the message.

As pastors, we receive our affirmation from the congregation; our successes or failures are known by many people, not just by a handful in an office. As a result, we feel vulnerable to the pressure of public opinion. That explains the strong temptation to choose to meet the expectations of our congregations above the needs of our wives and children.

The pastor often feels as if he has many bosses. But keeping all of them happy will drive him to ignore the feelings of those he dearly loves—those who will, at least for a time, put up with neglect.

To reinforce our conviction that the family is more important than the congregation, every one of us ought to make some hard, deliberate choices in our families' favor. We should take them out for ice cream rather than attend a finance committee meeting—at least once! Spend an evening on a family project rather than attend the meeting of the Sunday school council.

I've tried to cut down on outside speaking engagements for the benefit of my family and the church. But often it's those small daily decisions that really tell whether we value our families above those who pay our salaries. Start today by making some tough choices in favor of your family.

Faithfulness is more important than competition. It's easy to get discouraged in the ministry when we compare ourselves with others. Members of our congregations compare us with television preachers or with the super-church pastor who is in his third building program.

Stories of successful ministries are legion. If we focus on them, we will soon be dissatisfied with our own part of the vineyard. We know we have overcome a spirit of comparison when we are able to rejoice in the success of those who are more gifted than we are. When we are content with our little part in the total work of God on earth, we will have a sense of satisfaction and fulfillment.

Love is more important than ability. Obviously, we cannot function without gifts that qualify us for the demands of the ministry. We must know the Word and be able to communicate it. And we must have skills in leadership and working with people.

Yet, surprisingly, Paul gave those essentials a lesser place than the quality of love. Speaking with impressive ability, exercising the gift of prophecy, having the faith to move mountains, and even giving all possessions to the poor—to do all these without love is folly (1 Corinthians 13:1-3).

Of course, love in itself would not qualify us to shepherd a congregation. But Paul would tell us we ought to concentrate on love. When faced with a choice, we ought to develop the ability to love rather than the ability to minister.

Even the best Bible teaching does not change lives if it's not filtered through a personality filled with love. When we preach against sin harshly, we seldom motivate the congregation to godliness. But when we preach with brokenness and love, the Holy Spirit melts hardened hearts. We cannot say it often enough: without love, we are nothing.

For many of us, at least half of our ministry is over. You will never pass this way again. If your priorities are misplaced, now is the time to get your house in order.

Look over your week's schedule and ask what you would change if you lived it according to God's priorities. When a famous sculptor asked how he made an elephant, he answered, "I take a block of marble and cut out everything that doesn't look like elephant."

Take that block of time and cut out everything that isn't top priority. List your activities based on comparative worth.

By deliberately choosing to give more time to those things God thinks are important, we will probably find that we are accomplishing as much as ever. When we seek first the kingdom of God and His righteousness, our productivity does not cease. Only then do we give God an opportunity to add to our ministries other matters that formerly were our primary concerns.

If our priorities aren't straight, our ministries won't be either.

18
Failure:
Why Does It Sometimes Happen?

I talked recently to a discouraged pastor. His deacons were not supporting him, the congregation was apathetic, and his wife was complaining about his salary.

He was searching for an honorable exit, a way to resign with dignity. He planned to apply as a salesman with a firm that he had worked with before seminary.

What constitutes failure? Was that pastor a failure? The answer depends on one's perspective.

There are at least two kinds of failure. We can fail in the eyes of men. That hurts our egos. Those of us in public ministries are observed by many people; there's no such thing as resigning "quietly." And unless we move to larger churches, we're often viewed as failures.

Of course, it's possible to fail in the eyes of men and succeed in the eyes of God. The prophet Isaiah was called to be a failure (Isaiah 6:1-13). If you measured his ministry by statistics, he would not win the Most Outstanding Prophet award.

But the reverse is also possible: we can succeed in the eyes of men and yet fail in the sight of God. In this second kind of failure, we may tell ourselves that our success is for the glory of God, but the hidden motive may still be self-aggrandizement.

That leads to a question: Is it possible to be called by God and yet fail in our calling? Yes. That's what happened to the disciples in Luke 9.

The failure of the disciples. Peter, James, and John had just come down from the mount of transfiguration with the Lord Jesus Christ. A crowd of people had gathered to watch the disciples free a boy from demonic enslavement.

The boy's father ran toward Christ, shouting, "Teacher, I beg You to look at my son, for he is my only boy, and behold, a spirit seizes him, and he suddenly screams, and it throws him into a convulsion with foaming at the mouth, and as it mauls him, it scarcely leaves him. And I begged Your disciples to cast it out, and they could not" (vv. 38-40).

There you have it—failure in the ministry. As any preacher knows, it's tough to get a crowd; and when you've got one, you'd like to be at your best. But though the disciples wanted to see God glorified, they couldn't perform the miracle. The crowd was about to leave disappointed.

Let's give the disciples credit for trying. Some pastors would never even attempt to cast out a demon. At least the disciples exposed themselves to the possibility of failure. They did not back off.

Yet they failed. Did they go beyond their calling? Were they "out of the will of God"? No. Earlier, in the same chapter, Christ had called the twelve, and He "gave them power and authority over *all* the demons" (v. 1, italics added). They should have been able to cast out this disobedient demon.

But at this moment their call was ineffective, their commission wasn't successful, and their authority didn't work. Why? Three reasons come from the text.

Reasons for their failure. First, they lacked faith. Christ answers them, "O unbelieving and perverted generation, how long shall I be with you, and put up with you?" (v. 41).

Christ calls them unbelieving. Whatever the cause, they didn't have faith for this particular miracle.

We as pastors can identify. Almost every problem in the congregation eventually comes to our attention. We see divorce, moral failure, and personality conflicts. Under the weight of such discouragements, it's easy to entertain doubt.

"If Christ's power is so great, why doesn't He heal this marriage? Why doesn't He . . . ?" At that point, we're on the verge of being spiritually paralyzed, unable to fulfill our calling. Without faith, we are powerless.

Second, they lacked discipline. In the parallel passage in Matthew 17, Christ added, "But this kind does not go out except by prayer and fasting" (v. 21).

The disciples' authority was not automatic. Just because they had cast out demons in the past did not mean they could count on such authority in the future. Their calling would have to be renewed by fervent prayer and fasting.

Maybe they were too busy for a time of spiritual refreshment. They may have begun to live off their own success stories and think they were too busy for the basics.

We're not very adept at fasting. Warren Wiersbe says, "Call a feast and everyone is there. Call a fast and nobody shows." Without discipline, our ability to function spiritually is jeopardized.

Third, they lacked humility. They asked a question we hear repeatedly in our day: "Who is the greatest in the kingdom of heaven?" (Luke 9:46). Who has the greatest church, the greatest Sunday school? Who is the greatest preacher, the greatest author?

Those questions reveal a carnal sense of comparison. On a dark night, we can argue about which star is the brightest, but when the sun comes out it makes no difference—all stars fade in its brightness.

Paul said that those who "compare themselves with themselves" are without understanding (2 Corinthians 10:12). We don't know who the greatest preacher is. That's for God to judge. When we stop comparing ourselves with ourselves and compare ourselves with Christ, we find that there isn't much difference between us.

The disciples' pride led to a spirit of criticism also. They tried to prevent someone else from casting out demons in the name of Christ "because he does not follow along with us" (Luke 9:49). This person was successful in the very ministry in which they had failed. Like us, they tended to be suspicious of those who were succeeding in the task where they were floundering.

God often uses people who don't agree with me. My pride has occasionally prevented me from rejoicing in the success of those who don't belong to my denomination or who differ from my theology.

Reasons for our failure. Today, people still gather to see a display of Christ's power. They want to see drug addicts converted and marriages saved. They want to hear songs sung with joy and the Word preached with power. But unless we have faith, discipline, and humility, we will not be able to fulfill our calling.

We'll say to this mountain, "Be cast into the sea," or we will command the demon, "Be gone in Jesus' name." Neither will budge, and the crowds will leave disappointed. We know we were called, but our authority has evaporated. We've failed in God's work.

Maybe my pastor friend who is planning to become a salesman wasn't called to be a pastor. Or maybe he's in the wrong church.

Then again, he might be in the will of God but passing through a desert experience. He just needs someone to encourage him, to let him know that he is appreciated.

Or perhaps he has taken his calling for granted and has begun to live off substitutes. It may be that he has lost his authority, not his calling. That's why the mountains aren't moving and the demons refuse to leave.

I've learned that when I cannot exercise my authority to minister, God is calling me back to the basics. Faith, discipline, and a humble spirit can restore us to the place of blessing. Even commissioned disciples fail when they take their calling for granted.

19

The Fallen: How Can We Reach Out and Restore?

A seminary professor once told his students that they should become familiar with a vocation other than preaching because a certain percentage of them would eventually fall into immorality and have to leave the ministry. Although we might cringe at such advice, the professor was probably right.

A few months ago when I heard a friend had to resign because of adultery, my reaction was, "He's the last person I'd expect that to happen to." But, unfortunately, the last is often the first.

The high price of sin. Recently I asked some evangelical leaders whether a man who had fallen into sexual immorality should be restored to the pastorate. They said it's possible but highly unlikely.

An elder is to be "blameless" or "above reproach" (1 Timothy 3:2). It's difficult to regain the public trust and to rebuild a reputation destroyed on the rocks of infidelity.

I believe, however, that Paul's standards in that passage refer to the present spiritual condition of an elder. For example, he is to be "free from the love of money" (v. 3), but that doesn't rule out the possibility that he did love money at some time in his life.

These qualities refer to a man who has grown spiritually and put his past life of sin behind him. It seems reasonable that if a man falls into sexual sin, repents, and submits himself to the discipline of his church, he could once again be "blameless," because he had dealt with his sin in a biblical manner.

With that in mind, I asked the same leaders if their church or denomination would ever call as a pastor a man who had fallen, but over time had demonstrated the fruits of repentance.

Again, they answered no, unless many years had elapsed, and the matter was long forgotten. Some knew of cases, however, where a man was restored to an effective pulpit ministry, but his congregation did not know about his past.

The apostle John defined three root sins: pride, covetousness, and lust (1 John 2:16). Yet we generally overlook the first two. Only the third has a lasting stigma.

Perhaps moral failure really comes from pride. Martin Luther wrote, "God frequently permits a man to fall into or remain in grievous sin so that he may be put to shame in his own eyes and in the eyes of all men. Otherwise he could not have kept himself free of this great vice of vain honor and a famous name if he had remained constant in his great gifts and virtues" (*Luther's Works: The Christian in Society I*, vol. 44 [Philadelphia: Fortress, 1966], p. 45).

But regardless of how offensive pride is to God, sexual sin is in a class by itself. Paul wrote, "Flee immorality. Every other sin that a man commits is outside the body, but the immoral man sins against his own body" (1 Corinthians 6:18).

Sexuality is such an intimate part of our lives, we cannot fail here without guilt and shame. In adultery, there is also the constant reminder of the consequences of sin in someone else's life.

Sexual sin is usually accompanied by other sins. A person who commits adultery breaks at least five of the Ten Commandments. He puts his desires above God, steals, covets, bears false witness, and breaks the explicit commandment "You shall not commit adultery."

Because of the shame of sexual sin, there is an overwhelming tendency to commit other sins to cover the deed. If someone had told King David he would get a man drunk and eventually have him murdered, he wouldn't have believed it. Yet sexual sin made him a liar, thief, and murderer.

One denominational leader who had investigated a number of instances of alleged infidelity said he was surprised at how often pastors would lie, even invoking God's name, in covering their sin. Yet we shouldn't be surprised. If a man can violate one of God's clearest commandments, other sins come easily.

A person who falls also tends to develop a pattern of infidelity. One pastor's wife complained that her husband was unfaithful not only in their first church but also in each successive pastorate. He kept believing he could get by because no one was willing to blow the whistle.

Sexual sin is a serious offense. Nevertheless, too often we force a man to the sidelines because of a single immoral act that we refuse to forgive and forget. There are former pastors who have genuinely repented and have accepted the discipline of the church. Even if they cannot be restored to the pastorate, they could be used effectively in related ministries.

The possibility of restoration. In Galatians 6:1, Paul answers the questions we might have about restoration: "Brethren, even if a man is caught in any trespass, you who are spiritual, restore such a one in a spirit of gentleness; each one looking to yourself, lest you too be tempted."

What does it mean to restore one who has fallen? The Greek word *kataritzo* was also used to refer to setting a broken bone. Unfortunately, many bones in the Body of Christ have remained out of joint and have never been restored.

In a typical case of a pastor who commits grievous sin, he resigns almost immediately, has nowhere to go, and is forced to leave the area. Often his salary is cut off immediately with no provision made for his future.

Because of his shame, he does not seek the fellowship of his friends. They feel awkward about approaching him, so a curtain of silence falls around him and his family.

He feels ostracized, but his friends see his hasty exit as evidence that he is unwilling to face up to his deeds. Yet whether or not the man realizes it, his wounds need healing that only friends can give.

Paul also identified who should take the initiative: "you who are spiritual."

When someone falls into sin, the difference between carnal and spiritual Christians becomes clear. Under the guise of holiness, carnal believers will be critical, always demanding the maximum penalty.

One denominational leader told me that when a brother falls, some almost show delight rather than sorrow and remorse. The self-righteous believer uses the opportunity for self-exaltation, seeming to enjoy picking on a brother who has been wounded.

A group of pastors sat discussing the news that a fellow minister had resigned amid rumors of sexual unfaithfulness. Yet when one asked whether anyone had made contact with him, they were reduced to silence. No one had.

The truly spiritual believer will be grieved and ask how his comrade can be restored. It's not the fallen brother who should do the restoring; the initiative should come from sensitive, spiritual Christians. They will be willing to risk reaching out despite the possibility of being misunderstood and accused of being "soft on sin."

Finally, how should restoration be done? Paul said, "With a spirit of meekness" (KJV). If a person has a broken bone, he doesn't want it pushed into place with a crowbar. It needs to be set with gentleness. There is no room for condemnation or self-righteousness. We must be aware that we could commit the same sin.

If the brother acknowledges his sin and repents, then fellowship can be restored. That's the first step in the long healing process.

Eventually, he may be able to serve the Lord again in a different capacity. Let's not predict what God might do. Sometimes the bird with the broken wing does soar again.

Just because the devil has won a game, let's not concede the whole tournament.

20

The Church:
What Is Christ's Blueprint?

Whenever I'm asked, "Where is your church?" I'm tempted to answer, "On Sunday, it's at 1630 N. Clark Street in Chicago, but during the week, it is scattered throughout the entire Chicago area!"

The word *church* is never used in the New Testament to refer to a building but rather to the people of God, those who are "called out" by God to form the Body of Christ. It refers to saints on earth as well as saints in heaven. Those churches on hilltops with cemeteries around them are communicating a powerful theological lesson: the saints militant and the saints triumphant are all part of the same family. That's why the cemetery surrounds the church—you have to walk past the alumni association before you get to the undergraduates!

I think it was Reinhold Niebuhr who wrote that the church reminded him of Noah's ark—you couldn't take the stench within if it wasn't for the storm without! Whatever we may say of the church, this much is certain: it represents the highest priority on God's agenda and is His blueprint for completing His plans on earth. When Christ predicted the formation of the church, He highlighted certain features that we must return to again and again if we don't want to waste our time taking costly detours. His words are familiar: "And I also say to you that you are Peter, and upon this rock I will build my church; and the gates of Hades shall not overpower it" (Matthew 16:18).

If we understand the features of the church, we will be able to serve with freedom and joy. What do we learn about the church in this statement?

Christ owns the church. "I will build My church." Believers were purchased at high cost; understandably, we are God's property. If the value of an object is determined by the price paid for it, then we are valuable indeed. We are not purchased with silver and gold but with the costly blood of Christ. The cross of Christ is an everlasting testimony to how much believers are actually worth to God! Of course, He wouldn't have had to have Christ die for us. But in choosing to do so, our Lord affirmed that we are infinitely precious to Him.

The implications for our ministry are obvious. *God's people do not exist for their own benefit but for His benefit.* In our interpersonal relationships, we must remember that we are dealing with God's property, His people redeemed for His own purposes. That's why church leaders are exhorted to humility and not dictatorial leadership: "Therefore, I exhort the elders among you, as your fellow elder . . . shepherd the flock of God among you, exercising oversight not under compulsion, but voluntarily, according to the will of God; and not for sordid gain, but with eagerness; nor yet as lording over those allotted to your charge, but proving to be examples to the flock" (1 Peter 5:1-3).

There's no place for manipulation or coercion within the church. Certainly church leaders have to exercise authority as the Scriptures teach, but not with the hidden motive of making their ministries appear successful. All fund raising techniques and building programs must be scrutinized; hidden motives must constantly come under the microscope of God's searchlight. Why? It's because we are dealing with His people, His handiwork. Furthermore, we are accountable to one another. The leader who says, "I am accountable only to God," speaks arrogantly and ignorantly. He forgets that God expects mutual submission and servanthood from every member of the Body. *All* believers belong to the same family and have privileges and responsibilities.

Whenever I use carnal methods to accomplish worthy goals, I have forgotten who owns the church; whenever I am envious of those who are more successful than I, whenever I use the church to exalt my abilities or give the appearance of success, I have forgotten who owns the church.

What a relief to realize that the people in my congregation are God's property! Aren't you glad that those who stubbornly refuse to see your viewpoint don't belong to you? Like Moses, we must tell God from time to time, "Remember these are *Your* people!"

If you have never given your congregation to God, do so right now. You will find a new freedom to serve when you recognize God as the rightful owner of His people.

Christ builds the church. "I will build My church," Christ said. In all of our discipleship and evangelism we must realize that we cannot do Christ's work for Him. Before He left, He gave instructions to the disciples to "make disciples of all nations" just as He had done while He was on earth. Now we are His representatives, standing in for Him during this period of His physical absence from earth. He did not make disciples *en masse*, nor can we!

Several years ago, I attended a joint session of the National Religious Broadcasters and the National Association of Evangelicals, meeting in Washington, D.C. There were hundreds of displays exhibiting the latest in technology, all used to spread the gospel around the world. After walking through acres of equipment, I began to wonder how the early church ever made it!

They, of course, made disciples the hard way, one person pouring his life into another in "on the job" training. Since those believers could not rely on the mass media, they felt an obligation to witness with their own lives and lips to everyone who came across their paths. That's how the church was built, and that's how Christ intends that it be built today. We can be grateful for the Christian mass media, but there is no shortcut to building the church.

The stones for Solomon's Temple were cut in a distant quarry and then brought into the Temple area and assembled without the noise of a hammer. In Ephesians, Paul says that God is building a habitation and believers are the stones. He chooses those whom He will save and brings them into a relationship with one another and with Himself. He fits us into the building as it pleases Him. He is building a place in which He Himself will dwell. (Ephesians 2:20-22).

Building the church is not left up to us, though we participate in the process. Our responsibility is to find how Christ did it and then reproduce His methods. Recognizing that He is the primary builder gives us hope and courage in the building process.

Christ preserves the church. "The gates of Hades will not prevail against it," Christ said. This expression probably refers to His own impending death. The same description is used by Hezekiah in Isaiah 38:10 to refer to his own death. What Christ seems to be saying is this: although the gates of Hades will close behind Me, they are powerless to keep Me within their grasp. The advance of the church will not be halted by such apparent setbacks. The church is indestructible.

That ought to take some of the pressure off our schedules! We can be involved in building the church with a sense of trust, believing that God's ultimate purposes will be accomplished.

Paul says in Ephesians 2:20-22, "Having been built upon the foundation of the apostles and prophets, Christ Jesus Himself being the cornerstone, in whom the whole building, being fitted together is growing into a holy temple in the Lord; in whom you also are being built together into a dwelling of God in the spirit." Notice the three passive verbs that Paul uses to show that the church is both built and preserved by God. We "having been built" are also "being fitted" and again are "being built together into a dwelling of God in the Spirit." Believers are being acted upon by God who is in the process of doing His work on earth. Like the stones referred to earlier, God is using His chisel and hammer to ready the church for His own purposes.

What an encouragement! To be involved with Christ in the building of the church is a no-risk venture. Eventual success is guaranteed.

Peter Marshall said, "It is better to fail in a cause that will eventually succeed than to succeed in a cause that will eventually fail." Think about the implications: though we may fail in many ways, we are embarked upon an enterprise that has God's highest priority, and eventual success is inevitable. The gates of Hades will not prevail against it.

Christ empowers the church. To Peter Christ said, "I will give you the keys of the kingdom of heaven; and whatever you shall bind on earth shall be bound in heaven, and whatever you shall loose on earth shall be loosed in heaven" (Matthew 16:19). Later, Christ gave the same authority to all the apostles.

Here Christ is giving the apostles power to carry out their assignment. It's unthinkable that He would give the disciples a blueprint and not give them the ability to carry it out. If I send my child to the store to get some groceries, I must give her the money to buy the items. Whether the list is long or short, whether it is costly or cheap, she must look to me for the resources to pay. Christ must give resources to those who would work with Him in building the church. Because all authority has been given to Him, He can say to us, "Go ye therefore."

The church is God's number one priority in the world. It displays His wisdom, both now and in the ages to come "in order that the manifold wisdom of God might now be made known through the church to the rulers and authorities in heavenly places. This was in accordance with the eternal purpose which He carried out in Jesus Christ our Lord" (Ephesians 3:10-11).

Christ has not left us alone. He resides in us and works with us in the building of His church. When Augustine was told Rome had been sacked, he reportedly said, "Whatever men build, men will destroy . . . so let's get on with building the kingdom of God."

Since whatever men build, men will destroy, let us get on with the business of building the church, for our Lord has promised that the gates of Hades cannot prevail against it. No risk is entailed. We have His promise of eternal success.